Topaz Publishing

READING ENTERTAINMENT
FOR THE ENTIRE FAMILY

Cover Art: Dawne Dominque Copyright

December 2011

Editor: Kase J. Reed

Line Editor: Topaz Publishing

ISBN: TPEB000000019

ISBN-13: 978-0615627762
ISBN-10: 0615627765
WC: 31,776

Genre: Topaz Whisper, Inspirational

Topaz Publishing, LLC

USA

It' Sunday!

Inspired by the Life of
Sunday Stepney Lewis

At her Grandmother's behest, Sunday's weekday name was given. Born last of nine siblings, Sunday refused to hide her powerful singing voice among her talented brothers and sisters. A bratty little girl grows up and paves her way through the cruel music industry. Along her journey, she finds heartache, pain, triumph, and lastly redemption. It's Sunday, by Sunday S. Lewis, Topazpublishingllc.com

Available in E-Book, Print & Kindle

Thank you for buying a product of Topaz Publishing
Quality Reading for the Entire Family

It's Sunday!

Inspired by the life of

Sunday S. Lewis

By

Sunday Stepney Lewis

It's Sunday!

Dedications

To my Loving Family and Faithful Friends

Thank you for your love and support.

In Memory

Beloved Father, R. L Stepney

Beloved Brother, Alvin Lee Stepney Sr.

Acknowledgements

Vernard Johnson, Producer

Bert Cross, Producer

Co-Author, L.J. Maxie, Topaz Publishing

Table of Contents Page

It's Sunday!

Sunday Stepney Lewis

CHAPTER ONE
Beginning of the Day

In the beginning, God created the heavens and the earth. Then he made, Sunday. I don't mean Sunday, the first day of the week. I mean Sunday, the person—a skinny, big cheeked, spoiled little brat of a girl—a shy, innocent, five year old with big glasses.

All my life, I dealt with the weekday jokes. Songs like the theme from *Happy Days,* the television show—you know, *Sunday, Monday, happy days, Tuesday, Wednesday, happy days.* I've heard this refrain all my life, which was not always a terrible thing.

On the first day of school, I would cringe with embarrassment when the teacher called the attendance roll. "Who Is Sunday?" she'd say, looking over the top of her glasses.

Hearing her question, I knew the moment of truth had arrived. I'd push my glasses on my nose; raise my hand timidly, and shout, "Here!"

It's Sunday!

With a name like Sunday, it was obvious the entire class was curious. Snickers echoed in the air as I waited for their crude comments; I was never disappointed. Everyone was watching me. Laugher erupted behind the cloud of utter confusion. Just as I had expected; there it was, someone was bouncing in their seat singing the days of the week.

When my parents gave me this unique name, God also gave me a wonderful sense of humor. Had he not, I could have easily felt people were making fun of me. This odd little girl sat in the third row with neatly pressed hair and pigtails askew. Even then, I drew attention. Was their behavior admiration, ignorance, or sheer meanness? At any rate, I grew to love the response my name evoked.

Was I in training for my destiny? Would I someday hear my name blasted from a microphone, then relish the strident cheers of my adoring fans? Yes, even then, I knew I was different. I wanted to be a singer— not just any singer. I wanted to be the best.

Everyone thought it was cute to sing the days of the week song to a toddler. While they bounced me upon a friendly knee, their melodic gesture encouraged me to sing. Therefore, I had a no fear attitude when it came to singing. To this end, I gained many friends who showered me with praise.

* * * * *

Whether living in a mansion, or a shack, most people feel a preacher's home should be clean and tidy. Cleanliness is next to Godliness, so they say. Members of their household should be well behaved. Then, there are those who believed a preacher's home is a place of total chaos and unpredictable events.

Of course, the home environment should be sacred. Scripture, songs, and praises of worship should be wafting from the rafters 24/7.

Because of all these beliefs, my mother taught bible lessons to her offspring, while our father took pride in teaching us to sing.

Often, we would entertain guests or other relatives; by popular demand.

It's Sunday!

"Where are the kids?" they'd ask. "We'd love to hear them sing before we leave."

Their hopeful requests were always filled. With a strong voice, my father summoned his seven children. Then, standing in the living room, my father would pat the side of his trousers. ♫"Come and gather around me," he sang.

♫"Come and gather around," we'd repeat, rushing toward the lure of my dad's familiar call. No matter what we were doing, my daddy's call was music to our ears. We'd drop whatever we were doing, and heed his call; clamoring like seven chicks to a mother hen.

Watching us sashay into the room, Dad's eyes would narrow into a playful glint. A warm smile would tug at his lips. While he stamped a rhythmic beat on the hardwood floor, his authoritative voice commanded his brood to assemble. ♫"Come gather around, and sing praises to the Lord."

Being the runt of the group, I'd attempt to gather, but to no avail.

There was simply no room for me. I'd poke my head between my older siblings, only to be pushed aside. Try as I might, there was no space for one so small. My persistence was often reprimanded with their stern facial expressions. Plus, all of the harmony parts were taken.

Our guests would smile as they watched the joyous spectacle. They'd nod their heads, tap their feet, clap their hands, and sometimes they'd sing along. Though we were doing what came naturally, I learned at an early age, our singing brought pleasure to the masses.

* * * * *

Keeping our attention during bible lessons was difficult at times. A ringing phone would come to our rescue, and even if we had company, we had to endure what we felt was sheer torture. I remember one of my friends lying to get out of hearing the coveted bible lessons.

Nevertheless, people always requested that my siblings sing. From church gatherings, to family reunions, and after Sunday dinner, my family was expected to perform.

It's Sunday!

When our guests went home, our house returned to normal, then we'd return to our daily chores.

These gatherings were always fun, but they'd leave me upset. Because I was so young, I was never allowed to sing or practice with the older children. Instead, I'd linger in the same room, or follow my mother around the house as she completed her duties.

Helping mother was fine, but inside the house, the lure of harmonious notes tugged at my heartstrings. While washing dishes, mother would dunk her dishtowel, then run the soapy rag across a plate. Observing my scowl, she'd ask, "What's wrong, Sunday."

Looking toward the living room, I'd reply, "I know the words, Mama. I can sing too."

"I know honey, but it takes time to learn a new song. If you come in too soon, you could mess up the entire thing."

"I know the words. Why won't anyone believe me? I can sing."

Mama patted me on the head. "I know. And someday you'll be the best."

"Jaden doesn't know all the words. Daddy is letting her sing. I know she doesn't know the words, because I heard her sing."

"Honey. She'll catch on."

"But Mama. It's not fair. Why do I have to stay in here, while they're in there having all that fun?"

"In time, Sunday. All in due season."

"It's my due season now," I insisted, "and, I want to sing."

When I was fretful about singing with the group, mother always knew how to comfort me. "In due season, the trees will blossom and bring fruit. You understand that, right?"

I nodded. "Yes, but I'm not a tree."

"In due season, you'll blossom like those fruit trees in the country. Then, you'll bring forth fruit." Mama warmed her dishwater as we talked. "Now, if you try to pick a plum and its green, it won't taste very good. It will be tart and bitter."

It's Sunday!

With innocent eyes, I asked, "Are you saying I'm not ripe enough to sing, Mama?"

Mama stifled her laughter. "Well, not exactly. You can sing praises at any age. But, to sing with the group, your voice needs to mature just a bit."

"Oh. I understand. Tomorrow, my voice will be mature enough to sing. Right?"

Mama smiled, plunged the teacups deep into the soapy water, then chuckled to herself. "Oh, Sunday. You're such a mess."

CHAPTER TWO
Have You Ever Seen the Devil?

Every morning, I'd wake to the sound of my mother as she prayed in the privacy of her bathroom. Her day always started in communion with the Lord. She'd pray for family, church members, friends, and for the lost. "Lord," she'd say, "please keep them in your care. We need you, Jesus."

By hearing my mother start her day in prayer, I learned that prayer is the best way to start any endeavor; such as your day, a new life, or a relationship. Consulting God in every aspect of my life was engrained inside me.

After mother finished her devotion, she'd wake her children. One by one she'd call them to begin their daily chores. "Get up Sunday, Jerrica, Jelisa, Jaden. Get busy cleaning the house."

Because we were pre-teens on a mission, we'd usually be up late. Waking us from the comforts of our beds was not the easiest thing to do.

It's Sunday!

Mother's harsh instructions were important. She trained us to become responsible women. Of course, I shared a room with my sister, nine year old Jelisa. Being five years older, she didn't appreciate the company of a little sister. If I woke up before she did, I felt it was my duty to assist my mother by waking her. Jelisa always slept with her hand outside the blankets. I'd call, "Wake up, Jelisa! Mama said get up!" Shaking her shoulder was fruitless. Jelisa would simply shrug off my attempts. It was always necessary to try another strategy. I'd put my bare foot in the palm of her hand to aggravate her.

Immediately, she'd open one eye, then close it blissfully. With her face pressed against the pillow she'd ask, "Sunday, have you ever seen the Devil?"

"Nope!" Horrified by her question, I'd quickly remove my foot, and then scamper from the side of her bed. Had she been possessed by the devil? Why would she ask such crazy nonsense?

Later in life, I realized she was trying to scare me so she could get more rest—her plan worked. I'd leave her alone.

Jelisa was stern, and protective of her little sister. No one dared harm me. However, I was shuffled from room to room because of my inability to follow Jelisa's instructions. Her rules were not difficult, but for a curious mind, Jelisa's room was paradise.

Ten year old Jerrica and eleven year old Jaden shared a room. While Jerrica was the prankster in the family, or the life of the party, Jaden was sweet and kind. My sisters were good roommates and got along pretty well.

My brothers, Jonas and Drew, slept in the same room. They were responsible for taking out the trash and mowing the yard. Next to me, Jonas was one year older, and considered the baby boy of the family.

When my parents entertained company, Jonas always made a grand entrance, interrupting my parent's guests.

"Good afternoon," he'd say with hands behind his back. "Mama. Daddy.

It's Sunday!

Can I get some water for anybody?"

Naturally, Daddy would get upset. Jonas was out of place. "Veanna," dad would yell, "tell that boy to get somewhere and sit down. Get outta grown folks business!"

Mother, a gentler sort, always rescued Jonas. "He's just trying to be nice, R. L."

"Well he'd better be nice someplace else."

Hearing dad's displeasure, Jonas would scurry down the hallway and disappear from sight.

Nell, Trent, and Braden, were the oldest of my siblings. They had families of their own. Those remaining beneath my parent's roof always did what our parents expected — get up early, and be active. Although I was the youngest of them all, I was still liable for maintaining the same principles as the others.

* * * * *

Sometimes, mama and daddy would make runs to town to take care of business. They'd leave the oldest in charge, which was Jerrica at this time.

Jaden was older and had a car and a job. When mama and daddy pulled the car out of the driveway, the party would start.

Immediately, Jelisa turned the television from cartoons, to SOUL TRAIN. Soul Train showcased the latest music and the newest dances. Jerrica, Jelisa, Drew, and my cousin, Taylor, would jump in the middle of the floor to form a Soul Train dance line. *Dancing Machine* was one of our favorite songs. Jerrica did the penguin; Jelisa did a dance called the muscle. Taylor did the snake, while Drew did the robot.

Jonas and I observed their wild behavior, as we were all supposed to be cleaning the house. After a period of time, Jonas couldn't take it anymore. He'd cry out,"Imma tell mama, when she gets home. Y'all know y'all not pose to be dancing!"

Those words always caught anger from Drew. He'd run toward Jonas with his fist curled. "Jonas, you shut up, before I put my fist in your mouth!"

It's Sunday!

Knowing Jonas' weakness, Drew would goose him in his side, just to aggravate him.

Jonas cried all the more. "Imma tell Mama!"

Intrigued by the comradely, I sat quietly, observing everything that was taking place. Impressionable and curious, I learned all I could from my older siblings. Many personality traits and characteristics were thrown in my path. Although I was the youngest, I had developed my own unique personality. At times, I was quiet and shy. If I felt comfortable, my nature was more imprudent.

Naturally, I'd place my two sticks on the fire. "Jonas, you're such a tattle tale. Mama's little baby. Stop crying before I goose you, too." I'd threatened Jonas with an outstretched finger. "Goosey! Goosey!"

Jonas was cramping my style. How was I going to learn to sing with Jonas making things difficult?

Dressed in the latest fashion of the 70's, Soul Train singers would confidently grasp the microphone, then make singing appear as natural as breathing God's good air. There was something about their performances that made an impression in my mind. I just had to do this.

It's Sunday!

CHAPTER THREE
Plastic Buttons~Talent Show

First grade presented my first singing opportunity. I was going to try out for the first grade talent show. Ms. Yearout was my teacher. "Alright students," she announced, "the first of September, we have an upcoming talent show. Anyone interested in trying out, please raise your hand."

I was first to volunteer. "Yes, ma'am, I would." Although I was withdrawn and shy, the thought of singing brought boldness to my timid heart. After class, Ms. Yearout took our names, and then gave us a parent consent form. This was a once in a lifetime shot. I could visualize standing before my audience while hails of clapping took on the sound of thunder.

Of course, I'd wear my pink dress with the dainty rosettes. Taking a bow, I'd curtsy, fanning my dress in the fashion of the great prima donnas.

There was no way my parents would deny my dream. A grin stretched from ear to ear.

Within a few weeks, my day had arrived. Tryouts were held in Ms. Yearout's classroom. Students were lined up outside the door. Each one paced, clearly anticipating their chance to win the grand prize. A shiny new bike, decorated with a large red ribbon, was just what I deserved.

Outside the closed door, we stood in line and waited. Contestants needed privacy during tryouts. After being told to remain quiet, we still prattled like magpies. Though nervous, each one expected to be chosen.

The judges consisted of three teachers, and two staff members. A little girl named Lisa, stood in front of me. She was fair skinned with long curly hair. Because she was well dressed and popular, Lisa's bright eyes were admired by staff and students. From where I was standing, I could smell her confidence.

Other students knew her talents well. Their whispers met my tender ears. "Isn't that Lisa?" I heard one say. "I know she'll win. That girl can really sing."

It's Sunday!

Finally, Lisa's name was called. Without looking behind, she strutted toward the opened door, and past Mrs. Simon who was assisting with tryouts. As soon as the door closed, some of the students placed their ears to the wall in an effort to hear.

After a few minutes, the door opened and Lisa came out. She was beaming, which wasn't a good sign. After sweeping her eyes over my white shirt and jeans, she smirked, then jerked her head. Her long wavy ponytail brushed my glasses, and I flinched.

Mrs. Simon beckoned me forward, and my heart raced. Maybe I shouldn't have raised my hand after all. I didn't know tryouts would be so stressful. With insides trembling, baby steps moved my sneaker clad feet toward the designated singing area. Nervous to no end, I rocked from side to side biting my bottom lip.

As if they had a mind of their own, my fingers found the plastic buttons attached to my shirt. *Wow. Buttons*!

They were profoundly fascinating. What a wonderful invention—so handy to have buttons on my clothing. To my surprise, I actually had three buttons sewn on my shirt.

And my sneakers—I didn't know they were unlaced. How could I sing with my sneakers unlaced?

"Go ahead, Sunday," Ms. Yearout encouraged. "Don't be nervous. It's okay to sing. Sing, baby."

Teachers and faculty looked on impatiently. Was this a good time to tie my shoes? Would I pass out? Did I even remember the words to any song?

Waiting, Mrs. Simon tapped her pen on her clipboard. It echoed throughout the classroom. The judges turned their eyes and looked at the other. Then, Mr. Jones shrugged. "Anytime now, Sunday."

A knot drew my stomach tight. Was now the perfect time for a restroom break? I had to think of something. Their lips were drawn. It was obvious these people were not impressed with my impression of a chicken.

It's Sunday!

I inhaled, and then placed my foot atop the other. *Think Sunday. Pretend you're at home in the bathroom mirror.* A wave of nausea came over me. I held my stomach visualizing myself as I stood atop a stepstool in my bathroom.

With hairbrush to my lips, I sang loud and clear. Yes, the bathroom was my sanctuary. It was my turn to shine. The shower curtains were the perfect accent for my grand performance. I'd gaze in the mirror, while perfect lyrics flowed from my lips. The angels in heaven were applauding, of that I was sure.

Of course, my father had a problem with my singing. He loved his evening television shows.

After a few bars of my favorite song, I usually heard, "Sunday! Shut your mouth, or close that door. I don't care which one you do.

I can't hear the television with you screaming!"

Close the door—are you kidding? The acoustics were perfect. My voice was so lovely against the bathroom walls.

How could dad not appreciate my God given talent? Notes floated toward the ceiling, then wafted over me like sprinkles of sunshine and daisies. "Okay Daddy. I'll close the door!"

After climbing from my perch, I'd close the bathroom door. Then, I'd reclaim the awaiting stool.

Eyeing myself in the mirror, I pondered. How could a man with such a discriminating musical ear, choose a television program over my beautiful singing voice.

Now, it was time to put my private practice, or screaming as my daddy called it, into action.

"Sunday." Mrs. Greenly raised her voice to get my attention. "Today, sweetheart."

Startled by the sound, I gasped. Mrs. Greenly had invaded my daydream.

Now, it was time to introduce the world to *my* talent. I parted my lips and forced out the words, ♫"One of these mornings. It won't be very long—. You will look for me—and I'll be gone."

Before I reached the next verse, the judge's mouths fell open. They looked at the other with widened eyes. Some of the faculty members started to laugh. As if teleported to a church setting, they started rejoicing and praising God.

Ms. Yearout's face brightened. She nodded. "Alright, Sunday. That's enough baby. I'm sure you've made it." With the staff in an uproar, she pointed to a package at the end of the table. "Give that to your parents. We'll need more information as well as their approval."

I picked up the package, turned to look at the judges, then walked toward the exit. Mrs. Simon was standing by the door. She opened it, then clapped her hands. "Good job, Sunday."

Behind me, the judges talked among themselves. Judging by their gleeful expressions, they were pleased.

* * * * *

On the day of the talent show, Lisa Johnson's parents came to support her. She sang a song, while the audience screamed with excitement. Her vocal abilities were outstanding.

Tinged with jealousy, my shoulders grew tight.

Next, the announcer cast her eyes toward me. "Now we will have little Miss Sunday Stepney. She'll come in her own way. Give her a hand!"

The audience clapped. I turned my eyes toward the row of stairs that led to the wooden stage. With each step, it seemed as if the stairs sprouted another step. Finally, I reached the top of that mountain, then looked at the waiting announcer.

How was I possibly going to outdo Lisa? She was good, and I was nervous. The announcer patted my head, and then gave me the microphone. After taking my place at center stage, I looked toward the ceiling to focus my attention.

The audience went wild. Someone from the audience yelled, "Sang Sunday! You'd better sing that song girl!"

I did a second rendition of the song I performed during tryouts. ♫"One of these mornings. It won't be very long—"

It's Sunday!

Once again, the audience yelled, screamed, and shouted as if they were in church. After the song was completed, I took a bow.

The announcer asked that all the contestants come back to the stage to announce the winner. "And the first runner up is—put your hands together for Little Miss Sunday Stepney!"

The audience stood up and applauded. Then she announced the winner. "And the winner is— Little Miss Lisa Johnson! Put your hands together! These ladies have done a marvelous job!"

Although I was first runner-up, I was happy. Lisa Johnson stood on stage, held the certificate to the new bike, and threw butterfly kisses to the audience. Yes, she was good, but she had not seen the last of me. We would meet again.

Sunday Stepney Lewis

CHAPTER FOUR
Close-Knit Family

Through the years, my daddy moved us quite a bit. We traveled from Rowlett, Texas, to Greenville, Texas. Then from Greenville, to Garland, Texas, and then from Garland, to Dallas, Texas. God always made provisions for this man of God and his family. As children, we transferred from school to school. These transfers made it difficult for me to really get to know children my age. However, with few outsiders to add to the mix, we remained a close-knit family.

My mother's siblings lived down the road. During the summer, I'd walk, with bare feet, to visit them. Something about the summer freed my lungs. I'd sing to myself as I walked from house to house.

Little Mama, my grandmother, lived next door. Tiny, her youngest son, and his family, lived with her. Tiny raised chickens, cows, and pigs. His daughter, Letchie, was my best friend and cousin.

It's Sunday!

Letchie's mother would prepare breakfast, but first, she'd chase us out of the kitchen with a broom.

Little Mama had a friend — the Widow Dimple. Widow Dimple lived directly behind Little Mama. She was an odd woman with large moles on her face. Her husband, Jack, was a well digger, and the best at what he did. It was rumored that Jack fell into a deep well and died. At least, that was what I heard her say. At any rate, they found Jack at the bottom, in a broken heap.

Every morning, Widow Dimple would drink coffee with Little Mama. At church, Widow Dimple was the recording secretary. Though she was a large woman, she was prone to falling out under the spirit. Often, we wondered if she was actually faking.

Her spells were connected to the beat of the music. If the music hit her just right, Widow Dimple would pass out.

Little Mama had the nicest set of steps on her front porch. As a singing group, many songs were practiced or composed there.

On this Saturday morning, I was about to take the first step when I heard, "Lit, I tell you dat child is gifted."

"Who, Sunday?" Little Mama questioned. "All of them cherens is special."

Dimple shook her head "I know music, and I knows when I hears something that ain't natural. And that gal's voice ain't natural. She's too little for a big voice like that."

"Dimple." Little Mama picked up her coffee mug and peered over her glasses. "You been talkin' bout that gal since she was born."

"Well, you mark my word, Lit. That gal is gonna be somebody, someday. I done got old, and I might not live to see it, but mark my word."

Widow Dimple's words gave me chills. An eight year old should not have such pressure. I opened the screened door and stepped inside. "Good morning. Has Letchie gotten up?"

"Come here gal!" The Widow Dimple had one lazy eye.

It's Sunday!

As soon as I was close enough she reached for me with gnarled fingers. I backed up almost touching the wall. "I ain't gonna hurt you."

"Yes, Ma'am." Her left eye went any place it wanted, while her right eye remained stable. Even though I was scared to death, I raised my brows to show interest, and then focused on her good eye. "You called me?"

Widow Dimple stroked my shoulders. "You and Jonas gonna sing tomorrow at church?"

"No Ma'am." Then I stammered, "We're all going to sing."

As if she was outdone, Dimple placed her hand on her hips. "Now, that just ain't fair. Why can't you sing alone?"

I winced under her words. "Well, mama said I'm not ready."

"Well, you tell that mama of yours she better recognize."

Little Mama snapped at widow Dimple. "You hush up now. Don't be makin' that child disrespect her elders. Veanna might put a switch to that gal."

When I saw Letchie walking toward the kitchen dressed in shorts and a tee shirt, I grinned. Boy was I glad to see her.

* * * * *

During the summer, we also spent time with our other cousins who lived down the street. Sharon and Karen were fourteen, and identical twins. Most times, it was difficult to tell them apart. We fought, disagreed, and loved each other all at the same time. Family ties were all around us. Being older than I was, Sharon and Karen knew all about boys. By age twelve, I believed I was ready to talk about boys, too. I wanted to spend the night with them, because we had planned to call Marcus Miller. Karen had a way with people, so I had Karen ask my mama.

My mother knew her daughter well. "What are you all trying to do—call boys?" She folded her arm and raised a suspicious brow. "I guess so. Make sure ya'll stay out of trouble." Then she warned, "And stay off that phone!"

It's Sunday!

We all answered my mother at the same time, knowing well what we intended to do. As soon as my mother drove away, we ran inside the house and into the twin's room. Immediately, we jumped on their twin beds.

"Let's call Marcus," I suggested right away. "He is like, so cute."

Sharon agreed, and then told Karen, "Girl, today is his birthday. Get the phone. Let's do this."

Overall, I was well disciplined. However, my peers and older cousins brought out the dark side of me. Sharon handed me the phone. "Here. You call him." She gave me a slip of folded paper with Marcus' phone number written on it. I dialed the number.

The phone rang several times. Finally, a lady answered. I cleared my throat.

"Um, um—Can I speak to Marcus?"

The woman paused. "Who may I say is calling?"

I was so nervous; I started to hang up the phone. My cousins laughed in the background. "My name is, Sunday."

"Who?" she asked. "What's your Name?"

"It's Sunday, like the day of the week." I guess the woman was Marcus' mother, or something.

"Are you serious? Your name is really, Sunday?"

"Yes Ma'am. Is Marcus there?"

The lady, still holding the phone, started laughing. Evidently, she turned from the mouthpiece to address people in the same room. "Hey ya'll! Can you believe this girl is named, Sunday?"

"Sunday!" they echoed loudly. Then, I heard wild laughing in the background.

Marcus finally picked up the phone. "Hello."

♫"Happy birthday to you," I sang. "Happy birthday to you.

Happy birthday, dear Marcus. Happy birthday to— you—."

"Thanks, Sunday. Listen. Don't mind my family. They don't have it all. Please excuse them. I wanted to talk to you the other day, on the bus."

Hearing his words, I puffed my cheeks into a smile. "Really?"

"Yeah. But you were sitting at the front."

"I didn't even see you on Mr. Denton's bus. I guess it was too crowded, huh? There were no seats left." At this point, I was curious to know what Marcus wanted. Had he realized how adorable I was? Maybe he'd heard how talented I am. My answer came quickly.

Marcus hesitated. "I wanted to know if, if, if your cousin, Sharon has a boyfriend. If not, would you give me her number? I wanna ask her if she'd like to meet me at the fair on Friday night."

Hearing his confession, I gnashed my teeth and screamed. Afterwards, I gave the phone to Sharon and stormed out of the room.

* * * * *

Life in Dallas was very interesting. After school, we'd get off the bus and hang out. By age thirteen, I took advantage of my female friends. Why not? Everywhere I looked, I saw the makings for a singing group.

One day, my desire to sing got the best of me.

Singing in the choir, I felt I had the experience to teach others to sing as well.

All we were doing was talking about boys anyway. Jerrica, Jelisa and Jaden had their own friends. My cousins and neighbors would suffice when it came to making harmony. "Letchie, Sharon, Kim, Flo. Let me teach you guys a song I learned at church the other day."

Yes. The girls were bored enough to give it a try. After pulling each one aside, I sang a note. They repeated the note, and I placed them accordingly.

Much to my surprise, we blended with perfect harmony. Then, I taught the girls the words to the song. Within a few minutes, we had a singing group that could stop traffic.

Cars slowed down, or pulled over to listen. A group of on-lookers gathered across the street. With this encouraging behavior, I was quick to teach them another song.

"Hey," one woman called, "Do ya'll take requests?"

I blushed. "No Ma'am. We're not ready."

It's Sunday!

Making eye contact with each one, I addressed the young teens. "Girls. We sound really good." Excitement electrified my soul as I slapped palms with Kim. Somehow, I felt I was doing what I was born to do. "Maybe we should form our own group. We sound awesome!"

"Yeah," Letchie added, "we do sound good!"

The singing group, *Blessed,* was born that day. Later, each girl became a member of our church choir. We performed at a church rally, and blew the crowd away.

Sunday Stepney Lewis

CHAPTER FIVE
Sunday, The Preacher's Daughter

By age fourteen, I was pretty tired of people's expectations. Everyone felt that preachers' kids were the worst. Time after time, I heard stories of how daughters should carry themselves — in a respectable and Godly fashion. Their demeanor needed to be reserved. They had to be innocent of wrong doings, and respectable.

It was always necessary to dress in modest apparel. My closet was filled with calf-length skirts and dresses. Revealing the body was shunned, and any form of facial accent, and make-up was strictly prohibited.

Do all preachers' daughters grow up to be disorderly, naïve, unruly, and disgraceful? So, what's the difference between them and other teens? The answer is, accountability.

School was not my favorite place to go, yet it was expected of me, and every single day.

It's Sunday!

There were just days I didn't feel like going to school—which was almost every day.

What's a girl to do; school was mandatory in my household? When it came to getting my fair share of rest, I had adopted Jelisa's attitude. Anyone interrupting my sleep had to be of the devil.

After I'd gotten to my feet, getting me out of the house was the next hurdle. Daddy would say, "What's wrong with you this time, Sunday?"

My reply was always the same. "My stomach is shaking up and down. I think I'm sick."

Everyone within earshot would laugh at me. While they went about their business and got dressed for school, I'd whine all the more. "I don't know why y'all don't believe me. My stomach is shaking. It really is—just feel it!"

My daddy would shake his head. "Girl. Get your coat and get yourself out of this house."

By the time I arrived on campus, I was pretty much okay. In route to school, somehow, my father would make the shakes disappear. As he drove along, he'd sing a song, which always melted my fears. Most times, we'd sing together.

The kids at school could be cruel. I'm sure they thought I was a special nut case. "Can she talk?" they'd ask. Or, "Is she dumb or something?"

Because I was sneaky and mischievous, I'd think to myself, *Can you talk Stuppo? Maybe, I just don't want to talk to you!* Duh, the idea was to remain a mystery. I wasn't accustomed to a predominantly African American environment. My neighborhoods always consisted of mixed cultures. There was no way I wanted to bring attention to myself. Being a preacher's daughter, I wasn't accustomed to kids using profanity. Hence, I refused to talk. However, there were a few exceptions to this rule.

During lunch, a half-eaten burger rested on my lunch tray.

It's Sunday!

After stuffing a few chips into my mouth, I sipped my soda. A pair of dark jeans moved beside me and stopped. Expensive sneakers sat just below them. Immediately, I pushed my glasses on my nose, and then gazed upwards.

Instead of a hamburger, a chilidog lay sloppily on this guy's oatmeal colored lunch tray. On further inspection, I gazed into the face of a gorgeous male. "Is anyone sitting here?" he asked.

Stunned, I looked at my tray and shook my head. There was no way I was making eye contact with Shawn Davis. Shawn made my heart race and my palms sweat. I had watched him since the first day of school. He was a gangly teen, with reddish-brown curly hair. His tawny complexion, light freckles, and deep dimples complimented his Kool-Aid smile. This was the first time he ever acknowledged me. "My name is Shawn. Is it okay if I sit next to you?"

Nervous to no end, I frowned then wiped my nose with a napkin. "Sure."

Shawn placed his tray beside mine. "My cousin told me you were shy.

You know Jeff, right?"

I nodded, then took a sip of my soda.

"Jeff said you were talented. We're forming a band, and looking for talent." He tilted his head to one side; his thick lashes commanded my attention. "You know my dad don't you?"

I shook my head and continued to eat my lunch.

"Reverend Bright, at St. John's Church?"

Again, I shook my head. I had no idea what he was saying, but he sure did look pretty saying it.

"It doesn't matter. I play a few instruments at church. You know, like the keyboard, and the drums. We've been looking for new talent. On Friday night, we'll have our first rehearsal. Will you be able to come?"

Even though Shawn was handsome, I didn't want to seem desperate. "I'll need to check my schedule. Then I'll let you know."

Shawn nodded. "Well, can I get your phone number. Here, I'll give you mine."

It's Sunday!

A grin stretched across my lips. I was getting Shawn's number. What was the world coming to?

"I need to give you the address. I'll call you tomorrow—if that's alright?"

Taking my spoon, I dipped it in my chocolate pudding. "Yeah, sure."

As promised, the following day, Shawn called. After giving me all the details, I decided to help him. Every now and then, I saw Shawn in the hallway. He'd give me a wave as he walked past. Friday night took forever to come.

Eager to impress, I searched my drawers for something cool to wear. Shawn Davis was going to discover just how sexy I was.

With my hair in place, I slid on my tightest jeans, and stuffed my feet into high heel shoes. Though my feet were bad, Shawn would never know. A low cut blouse revealed pre-teen cleavage, and lastly, make-up enhanced my natural beauty. There was no way Shawn was ever going to forget me. Yes. I meant to take his breath away.

Sunday Stepney Lewis

On Friday night, my mom dropped me off at Shawn's house. Eager to get started, I rang the doorbell and waited. Soon, a woman opened the door. "Well, aren't you precious. Are you here for the rehearsal?"

"Yes, I am." She led me to the rear of their large house. Reverend Bright had designed a home studio in one of their back rooms. Other people were also waiting, which shocked me. A few, I knew from our school choir.

Then, I saw her. Lisa Johnson, my competitor. Lisa was one grade above me. Shawn was two grades ahead of me. Students and teachers were also there.

Lisa had won the talent competition that year, too. I knew I could hang with her, because I came in second, once again. Competing with Lisa needed to leave my mind. This was another day, and another time.

I tried to pretend I didn't see her. From across the room, she yelled, "Hey Sunday. Girl, what you doing here?"

As she did in first grade and middle school, Lisa looked me up and down.

It's Sunday!

Yes, I had changed. Sunday was grown up. Like the gentleman he was, Shawn had introduced me to his other guests.

"Oh, hey, girl," I finally acknowledged. "What are you doing here? Shawn asked me to help 'im with his project. "

Shawn's face beamed. He seemed surprised that I knew Lisa. Later, I learned that Lisa was the one who told Shawn's cousin about me. Fondly, she called me the shy girl, who could really blow.

Before long, Shawn asked for everyone's attention. "I need the sopranos to my left, altos to my right, and tenors in the middle. And Sunday, you're lead vocal, okay?"

Taken aback by his request, I stammered. "M, me?"

"Yeah, you." There was a strange glint in his eyes. "Go over there."

Lisa slowly moved toward the alto section, while giving me an evil stare.

I chuckled to myself. She thought she was going to be lead singer.

Humph. Oh well, what will be, will be. I went to the studio microphone, then sang the words Shawn had given to me. Determined to get this part, I caught on to the words. After the recording session, everyone in the studio clapped their hands. Much to my surprise, they were giving me a round of applause.

From the corner of my eye, I noticed that Shawn's mother stood in the doorway and smiled. Yes. I had gained Shawn's approval, as well as his mother's favor.

The session came to an end. Shawn walked me to the car as I left to go home. For some reason, he couldn't keep his eyes off me. Fortunate for us, I felt the same.

My mom was not nosy. While she waited in the car, she read her bible instead of watching us.

Shawn slid his hands into his pockets. "I'll call you later — when everyone else leaves. We'll talk some more okay. We've got future plans for the studio. Alright?"

It's Sunday!

Once again, I nodded. This time, I smiled with widened eyes. "Sure. Okay."

Later that night, I waited patiently — expecting my phone to ring. Exhausted, I dosed off just as the phone rang. "Hello," I said, trying to sound cheerful.

"Hey, Sunday. I'm sorry for calling you so late. People kinda hung around. We decided to try another lead before making a final decision. We'll get back with you as soon as a decision is made. All right?"

Disappointed, I sighed. "Oh, okay."

"By the way, you have a very nice singing voice. I'd love to stay in touch. If that's cool with you?"

Although I was sleepy, alertness burst from my throat. "That's fine. Just keep me posted. And yes, I'd love to keep in touch."

I was disappointed that a decision had not been made. But, I was more excited to know Shawn would call me again. Before I heard from Shawn again, my daddy made a decision to move to another city. God had given him a vision to organize another church.

CHAPTER SIX
Uncle Hammy~A Broken Promise

Rowlett, Texas was country living pure and simple. Because most of our relatives lived so close, every day was special. My fathers' sister, Aunt Leola, lived right across the street, as did my mother's brother.

Aunt Leola often had wiener roasts in her front yard. On the Fourth of July, her husband, Uncle Hammy, took us on hayrides. The couple owned a small café, H & L, which was positioned next to their house. It had the most important thing a café needed; chairs that swiveled. Much to our liking, they sold hamburgers, ice cream sandwiches, and sodas. When customers are mostly family, friends, and neighbors, there is not much profit to be made.

Uncle Hammy would sit on his front porch. He was a kindly old gent who took an interest in the community. People would walk up and down the road taking care of personal business, then they'd stop and chat with Uncle Hammy.

It's Sunday!

To everyone, this overall wearing gent was a big-hearted guy. Plus, Uncle Hammy loved kids. Often, he kept a treat tucked away just for his little heartstrings. Hammy's wisdom was easy to understand. If you had a problem, one of Hammy's wise sayings could see you through.

Sitting on the edge of his porch, he'd eat his supper, or shave down a walking stick for an ailing friend. While he worked, his dark skin would glisten in the evening sun. An old straw hat covered his bald head. His cheeks were often in constant motion. Though, medium in stature, Uncle Hammy loved to eat.

That afternoon, I rode my bike right up to Uncle Hammy's steps. "What cha doing, Uncle Hammy?"

"Why, good evening Miss Sunday. I'm fixing this piece to put on the truck." He held up a new rope. "Gotta get things ready for the hayride tomorrow."

"I'm going too, right?" I tightened my grip on the handlebars and stood astride my bike.

"You betcha. There's nothing like driving in the evening air, and listening to my little rabbits sing." I was well into my teens, but to Uncle Hammy, I was his little rabbit.

"Yeah. I love singing on a hayride." A mosquito landed on my ankle, which was perched on the raised pedal. With a quick move, I swatted it.

"Especially when ya'll sing, *Troubles of this World*."

I grimaced. "You like that old song, Unk? It sounds kinda sad to me."

Hammy lifted his brown eyes and gazed into the distance. "What seems sad to some, is soothing for others."

"You say some weird things, Unk. But I understand it."

He tied a knot in the rope, then wiped sweat from his brow with his forearm. "Why don't you sing a few verses for your old, Uncle Hammy?"

I didn't have a problem with singing, but I was getting too old. Singing for Uncle Hammy was fine when I was ten or twelve. "Well." I scrunched my nose.

It's Sunday!

"We'll sing it for you on the hayride tomorrow night. Okay?"

Hammy narrowed his eyes. "Promise."

"Sure, Unk. I won't forget, and I doubt if you'll let me."

"Alright now," he warned, shaking his finger. "I want you to sing it just like you did at church. No shortcuts."

"Okay, Unk."

Like most teens, I had good intentions of singing for Uncle Hammy, but Titus Briggs was seated on the trailer. Titus was fine. Whew! He had helped my uncle load hay on the flatbed. In return, Uncle Hammy let him ride with us the next day. There was no guy cuter than Titus Briggs. His rich brown skin was velvety smooth and flawless.

With eyes the color of snuff, it was difficult not to get stuck in his web. He was tall, but brawny for his age. No, we didn't sing Uncle Hammy's pitiful song. We kept the music upbeat and cheerful.

While I sat among the hay, I pretended I'd forgotten my promise to Uncle Hammy.

Although, inside the cab, his lips were curled into a broad smile. In my heart, I knew he was fine with my decision *not* to sing his depressing song.

The trailer was crowded with young relatives. Anxious to get Titus' attention, I sat among bales of hay, breaking straw into tiny pieces. Feeling rejected, I then tossed them from the truck.

Because Titus was closer to Jelisa in age, he hardly knew I was alive. Even so, I couldn't stop staring at this chocolate chunk. If I didn't win his attention soon, the hayride would be over. The community was small, but for some reason, Uncle Hammy took his time.

We took the scenic route, driving past the old home place then lastly the cemetery. Pointing, nodding, and grinning, Uncle Hammy seemed to enjoy every second.

* * * * *

The next day, I was faced with my deepest regret. That night, Uncle Hammy took ill. Aunt Leola took him to the hospital, and he never returned.

It's Sunday!

Instantly, our world was torn apart. Hammy was more than just a man; he was the very thread of the community. People gathered on the steps of his café. There was mourning—such as I'd never witnessed in my young life.

Through her grief, Aunt Leola still found the strength to accommodate others. Now, it was our turn to serve her. God had called her mate—His soldier, home.

Grief stricken, I sat on the sofa and recalled events from the night before. There was something strange in the air that night. Did Uncle Hammy know he was taking his last hayride?

Then, I gazed out the living room window. The spot on the front porch, where Unk once sat, was now empty. *To be absent from the body, is to be present with the Lord.* 2 Corinthians 5:8. So now, Uncle Hammy sat in the company of the almighty God.

As expected, the funeral was packed. People stood outside with no chance to get inside the church.

Fragrant, colorful flowers were plentiful around the building. It was difficult to walk past the casket for viewing. Since I'd been selfish, I was totally destroyed. Uncle Hammy had made a simple request of me. A prideful and silly teen, I had denied him this last wish.

Washed in guilt, I stood trembling when the viewing precession started. It didn't matter who was scheduled to sing, I had to sing for my Uncle Hammy.

Pushing people aside, I made my way to the microphone. On a mission, I owed no man an explanation for my actions. Once in place, I looked to heaven, wiped the tears from my swollen eyes, then opened my mouth. "God give me strength. ♪ Soon, I'll be done — with the troubles of this world — troubles of this world — trou — bles of this world. Soon I'll be done — with the troubles of this world. I'm going home — to live with my…"

Visions of Uncle Hammy loomed above me. I could feel his presence in the room. Yes, he was pleased.

It's Sunday!

They told me that the processional stopped. Everyone sat still and listened. I had no idea at the time, and I didn't care. Seeing the tear stained eyes of my precious aunt, no one else mattered. This was Uncle Hammy's song.

Sunday Stepney Lewis

CHAPTER SEVEN
Life in Greenville, Texas

Greenville, Texas held new experiences. Sunday after Sunday, the car hit the road packed with noisy children. Goodwill Missionary Baptist Church was our goal. My brother, Jonas would annoy me while riding to church. Regrettably, the car was uncomfortable and tight.

Often times, we stayed in Greenville for evening service. Some of the church members would take turns cooking dinner for my family. Driving back home to Rowlett was too far. Soon, I learned that Goodwill Church had the best cooks in Texas. Although their cafeteria was tiny, it was still cozy with lots of love from the associate ministers, and church family.

We would feast on fried chicken, macaroni and cheese, and mustard greens straight from the garden. There were pineapple, chocolate and strawberry cakes, direct from Sister Margaret's kitchen. Everyone pitched in to make our visit a success.

It's Sunday!

Members of the church always looked out for the pastor and his nine children.

* * * * *

The school talent show had been my first performance, however my first opportunity to sing at church came shortly afterwards. The Youth Director, Sister West, was looking for someone to participate in a program for afternoon service. In a frenzy to fill an open slot, she approached the church musician. "I need someone to do a solo this afternoon, right before the guest church takes the stand."

The musician didn't hesitate. "Why don't you get little Sister Sunday and her brother? I'm sure they'll enjoy it."

Jonas and I had been messing around with my sister's new piano. He taught himself to play a few songs. Now this was our opportunity to perform.

We were talking to the other teens when Sister West drew our attention. "Sunday and Jonas. I heard y'all have a duet you've been working on. Would you mind singing it this afternoon on program?"

Excited to launch out on our own we both answered, "Yes ma'am. We'll sing for you!"

After dinner on the grounds, evening service finally started. The Mistress of Ceremony asked the guest choir to take the stand. "First. We're going to have a duet by Brother Jonas, and Sister Sunday Stepney. The whole church clapped.

Jonas walked toward the front of the church and sat down at the piano. Confident that my time had come, I stood next to him, holding the microphone. He played a short introduction, then looked at me, and nodded his head.

♫"Yes, Jesus loves me. Oh yes, Jesus loves me. Yes Jesus loves me, for the bible tells me so."

My family, other church members, and guest, stood to their feet. Their enthusiastic applause encouraged us.

When we finished, Sister West patted my brother on the back, and grabbed me with a tight hug. "Good job y'all."

Since that first performance, Jonas and I were considered a duo.

* * * * *

It's Sunday!

The Goodwill church had a balcony. It was mysterious, dismal, and spooky. Most times, I was so terrified I had nightmares a witch lived behind the dark closed door. Sometimes, thumping noises came from the balcony, and it wasn't my imagination. I'd jerk my head upward hoping something horrible wouldn't tear through the door.

No matter what the preacher said, each Sunday my mind would gravitate toward that haunting area of the deserted balcony. Did the devil actually live there? Was there really a witch sowing discord among the congregation?

The closest thing to a witch was Sister Vera. From my observations, this woman had to be at least one-hundred thirty years old. Folds of wrinkles were hardened as they lay against her disturbingly light-skinned face. Huge jaws were always set, locked tight, and drawn. Many believed her hair was long enough to reach her thick calves. No one knew for sure, as she kept the heavy gray mass piled high on her head.

Much like her hair, her brows were also thick and gray. She had opaque cataracts, which gave her rounded eyes an eerie appearance.

Her dense nails were curved and long. Often, they were painted a bright shade of red. Because Sister Vera was overweight, she'd waddle from side to side when she walked. Instead of wearing orthopedic shoes on her bad feet, she always wore men's leather boots below her drab Sunday dress. When she'd walk past, Sister Vera left a distinct trail of vanilla extract.

Sister Vera's patience with children was short, and I was sure she hated teens. Perhaps, she was born an adult. She loathed people, and wanted no one to hug her.

While daddy preached, this woman would huff and puff as if she'd explode at any moment. Was the good word getting next to her? I heard that the devil would burst into flames if pierced by the Holy Spirit. Sister Vera was as close to evil as I dared to come.

It's Sunday!

No matter where I sat, I could still see her milk colored eyes. When I'd sing, she'd scowl, looking at me as if she wanted me to shut up, and if I didn't, she'd shut me up.

There was always a gripe behind every statement she made. Obviously, this woman had no peace.

Sister Vera was usually the last person to leave the church. Her car was parked behind the church building. We doubted she ever went home. There was always something else for her to do. After church, I'd watch to see if she disappeared behind the creepy door upstairs. Then, one day, she did.

With sincere expressions, Jaden and Jerrica had convinced me that Sister Vera was indeed someone I didn't want to cross. Whatever she had hidden in that room, she wanted no one else to know. Other members of the congregation were friendly and Godlike, but not Sister Vera.

* * * * *

Cindy and Wendy Simmons were the teenage daughters of Rev. Simmons. We all feared the room at the top of the stairs.

They knew I was more afraid of the balcony than anyone else. They'd stand on the dark stairs and dare me to knock on the door at the very top.

This day, choir practice was over. Sisters of the church stood chatting about the new song we'd just learned. Interested in what they had to say, I stood near my mother, while other teens disappeared in four directions.

Suddenly, I noticed Wendy was walking toward me. There was a strange gleam in her eyes. Pulling on my arm, she explained, "Cindy wants to ask you something. She's waiting at the stairway to the balcony."

The word *balcony* made me cringe. I hesitated, then looked at my mother who was occupied by their discussion.

"Come on girl," Cindy insisted, "she's got something important to tell you."

"Why can't she tell me down here?" The mere mention of that dreaded place, and my heart raced.

It's Sunday!

"She can't." Wendy leaned toward my ear, and whispered, "It's about a boy. She's waiting for you."

By jerking my arm, Wendy was getting my undivided attention. With curiosity peaked, I surrendered. "Alright. Alright. Don't pull my arm out of the socket." I followed her to the stairs. "Where is Cindy?"

Wendy placed her fingers to her lips. "She doesn't want anyone to hear. She wants you to meet her in the room upstairs."

Immediately, I folded my arms. "I. Am. Not. Crazy. Do I look like a fool?"

I lifted my eyes and noticed that the door to the room was ajar. "Is she really inside that room?"

"Yeah. Trust me."

"Tell you what." I sighed. "You go first, then I'll walk behind you."

"Okay." Wendy nodded. "I'm not scared." Wendy placed her foot on the first step, then the second step. She reached out to me. "Come on."

With knees knocking, I noticed spider webs matted along the hand railing of the steep stairs. Although I didn't like spiders, I placed my foot on the first step. Slowly, we scaled the stairs as I listened for any unusual sounds. Beneath the door, I saw a faint light sifting through a narrow crack.

When we reached the top of the stairs, I looked down on the sanctuary. Suddenly, the door opened. Both girls pushed me from behind. Before I could gather my thoughts, I was swallowed-up by the darkness of the evil room. My heart raced as I tried to adjust my eyes.

A man wearing a ski mask snatched my arm, then slammed the door behind me. "Don't cream," he said, holding out his hands. "Hey girl—don't cream."

His words were ignored. Out of my mind with fear, I let out an ear piercing screamed. A smelly hand came from behind and clasped my mouth.

Then, I heard the confusion of female voices behind the door. They called my name, their voices quavering with concern.

It's Sunday!

The man pulled the ski mask from his disfigured face.

Seeing something I couldn't understand, I screamed again. Suddenly, the door swung open. All of the women from choir practice were standing in the narrow hallway.

While Cindy and Wendy were scolded, they stood with saddened eyes, and heads bowed. "We're sorry," they told the sisters of the church.

Huffing and puffing, Sister Vera pushed her way up the stairs, and past the gawking crowd. With a straining growl, she slammed them against the wall as she stormed forward. "Leave my son alone!" she bellowed. "He ain't hurting nobody! Now, git on outta here. If I hada wanted ya'll to mess with him, I woulda let him out."

My shoulders dropped. So, Sister Vera was *not* a witch. She had a grown son, with special needs. To keep him safe, she had locked him inside the room at the top of the stairs.

She stroked the cheeks of this very scared man. "You alright, Herbert? That gal didn't hurt you none, did she?"

Herbert shook his head, then whimpered like a scared puppy. He wasn't a bad person. Born with a horrible cleft lip and clubfeet, he wasn't a bad person at all.

The older congregation remembered Herbert as a little boy. One day, he simply disappeared. To protect him, Sister Vera would get to church early, then lock Herbert in the room at the top of the stairs. When everyone was gone, she'd open the door, then take him home.

* * * * *

The trip to Greenville, Texas was taxing on our large family. Eventually, my father decided to purchase the house across the street from Rev. Simmons. It was close to the church, and because of Cindy and Wendy, I didn't mind the move. These rambunctious teens made my life exhilarating. I visited their house so often, it was almost as if I lived there.

It's Sunday!
CHAPTER EIGHT
A Lesson in Life~Garland, Texas

Garland, Texas, presented more new adventures. When I wasn't singing; people watching was my favorite pastime. On this particular day, Dee-Dee and I sat on the porch discussing what we were going to do with our summer. Dee-Dee was brazen, and out spoken, while my demeanor was a little more reserved.

As people walked by our house, Dee would frown. "Those people are always walking on your grass. I'll bet you won't tell *that* girl to walk on the sidewalk."

I sized up the girl, who walked with a swagger. Yet, she appeared to be in a hurry. She looked thirteen years old, and stood about five-one. With a constant scowl, she didn't look very friendly. Nevertheless, we were standing on *our* porch, so what could she do to us?

Now, I could show my new friend how brave I was. "Walk on the sidewalk, and not on the grass," I called.

Obviously, hearing my words, the girl stopped walking.

She slumped her shoulders, turned around, and gave me the meanest mug I'd ever seen. "What did you say?"

"I didn't stutter." I placed my hands on my hips. "I said, walk on the…"

Before I finished my statement, I noticed the girl was searching on the ground. Finally, she located a brick, which was decorating a flowerbed. She growled as she yanked it from the soil. With stiffened shoulders, she marched up to me. Brows were lowered, and her yellow teeth were clinched tightly. The girl didn't say another word. Unexpectedly, she raised the brick high into the air, then slammed it against my skull. Brick against bone, made a thunderous crashing sound.

Stunned beyond all reason, the blow to my head caused me to lose balance.

With arms flailing in slow motion, I fell from the porch, then tumbled toward the fragrant grass, I claimed I was protecting. I closed my eyes as a numbing pain jolted my head to one side. As my vision turned foggy, I saw Dee-Dee, my encourager, run inside the house.

It's Sunday!

How could I have listened to her? Soon I heard shouting above my head. "There she goes," Dee called, pointing toward the store. "She cut through the fence behind that house."

While I lay on the ground, I heard thundering footsteps as my siblings chased after the disturbed girl.

Like an eagle, her feet seemed to take wings, and they were unable to catch her. Nell stayed behind. Being my oldest sister, she wanted to make sure I was completely all right. She helped me to a seated position. "Don't you worry about her!" she said, gnashing her teeth. "We'll get her."

By late evening, we called off the search. Then came the moment of truth; mama came home.

When she learned of the attack on her teenaged daughter, she couldn't help but pamper me. After all, I was innocent, right?

Concerned for my wellbeing, everyone rallied around me. I had no idea getting a knot on my head could cause such a stir.

My mother was steeped in worry. There were no major bruises or scars, just a huge knot on my head. Then, I took advantage of the special attention I was receiving.

Holding an ice bag to my throbbing head, I lay on the sofa and looked at television. Now, was a good time to test the waters. "Mama, do you think I could have a slumber party next Friday? Dee-Dee didn't get a chance to stay. You know— because of what happened?"

Mama looked at me with sadden eyes, then stroked my hair. "I guess so, Sunday. But you can only have a few girls. You hear me?"

I agreed to her terms. "Yes, ma'am. A few teenage girls with raging hormones was all I needed to cause total upheaval and mass destruction.

Grinning, mother shook her head in agreement.

* * * * *

Would Friday never come? My friends and I waited in anticipation. To make a long story short, a girl I didn't like, and didn't invite, crashed my party.

It's Sunday!

Our parents were friends, and my mother had invited her. Debbie was a total downer as she tattled constantly. Disaster struck the minute she arrived. For some reason Debbie had a way of working everyone's nerves. If she wanted to be liked, this was not the way to do it. She followed my mother around the house, keeping her abreast of our every move.

We played games. Debbie told my mother they were too racy. When I tried to call guys, Debbie made sure my mother knew every detail of the conversation.

What good was getting a knot on your head, if you can't enjoy yourself after the pain? Debbie was all up in our business. My mother had shut down our fun several times. Finally, enough was enough. We decided to exclude Debbie from our activities. Perhaps, she'd get the message.

Dressed in her pajamas, Debbie walked behind. "Hey, do ya'll wanna hear some scary stories?"

"No!" we snapped, with smug expressions.

"Talk to the hand." I rolled my eyes with my hand on my hip. After ruining our evening, we decided to ruin hers. I turned to the one thing I knew my mother loved. My pink CD player was getting old; even so, it still had excellent speakers.

"Okay ladies. Let's form a singing group." I grabbed my hairbrush to use as a microphone. Dee-Dee grabbed a comb, and the others pretended to hold microphones.

Excluding Debbie, we stood in a line, danced, and sang in perfect harmony. Debbie sat on my bed with arms folded. She may have ruined our plans, but she couldn't ruin our fun.

* * * * *

A week later, I walked to the neighborhood store with Jerrica and Taylor. Then, I saw the girl who hit me with a brick. This time, I had back-up. If she wanted to fight, I was ready. Her methods had been devious and sneaky — hardly equal.

It's Sunday!

Now the playing field was leveled. I would play it cool. Rather than facing this crazy person, I whispered to Taylor, "That's that girl who hit me with that brick. "

Taylor shuddered. "Are you kidding?" She slammed her fist into her opened palm. "Let's get her." She lunged forward, and I stopped her.

"No. She sees me," I whispered. "We'll let her go."

Trembling, and with bulged eyes, the girl looked as if she'd sprint at any moment.

Enraged, I took a stance between my family members. With shoulders drawn, I pulled my fist by my side. Scowling, I lowered my brow, and bit my bottom lip to keep my cool.

Anger caused my heart to beat off sync, while wild thoughts ran through my mind. *Where's your brick now. You dizzy heifer. You wanna piece of me? Just bring it. I'll mess you up!*

Apparently, weighing her options, the girl jerked her head to the right, then to the left.

She was looking for a way out and I knew it. Leaving her purchase behind, she bolted for the door.

I've often wondered what happened to that girl. Was she a troubled teen? Was she abused at home? Today, I picture her sitting in some jail cell. It was clear the child had issues.

That day, I learned a valuable lesson. Never talk noise to strangers; and looks can be deceiving. If I had remembered my mother's teaching, I would have been friendlier. Perhaps, the girl could have benefited from a cheery hello, instead. Plus, I'm positive Dee would not have taken a brick for me. Lesson learned.

It's Sunday!

CHAPTER NINE
Mischievous Teen~Dallas, Texas

It never dawned on me that passing notes in church could be a distraction. From time to time, the usher would remind me to pay attention to the message. I had no idea the spoken word would prepare me to face my future.

Now, young adults, the youth occupied the rear of the church. Often, the usher would encourage us to move forward. We were told to do the usual: spit out our gum, put up our cell, and stop talking.

To me, Sundays were for meeting with family and friends. Morning worship was my favorite time, as we had much to talk about. Keeping us from discussing our Saturday night activities was just rude. Nevertheless, we were always giggling about something.

Each Sunday, Kim, Shonda, Flo, and I, occupied the seats closest to the door.

When a new, or cute guy came to visit our church; we'd get a horrible case of the giggles, and then, we'd watch him like a hawk.

Today, who would get the caramel babe, with his light brown eyes, and a smile as wide as Dallas? Females are sneaky, but I felt that since I was the pastor's daughter, I should be the first to extend the hand of *friendship*.

This time, I had a strategy. To get a jump on the other girls, I decided not to wait until church was over. Flo was more assertive and didn't mind going after the man she wanted. She had been known to make her move, after services. Weighing my options, I reached inside my purse, got a pen, and wrote a note to the guy. After folding the note neatly, I passed it to Kim, who was sitting directly behind him.

When Kim looked at me, I cast my gaze toward the gorgeous male, who looked a few years older. Immediately, Kim caught the hint, and nodded back.

It's Sunday!

The note read, *Hello. My name is Sunday, what's yours? I couldn't help but notice that you were watching me. Are you still in high school or do you attend college? I like your smile. Do you have a Girlfriend?*

Out of the blue, Shonda poked me in the ribs. "Girl. Look whose coming."

Sister Jackson, the usher, had been standing by the door. With a look of utter disgust, she stepped gingerly down the aisle toward us. Sister Jackson was the meanest usher of them all. If there was such a thing as usher police, Sister Jackson had to be it. With lips flattened, she stood at the end of the pew. Tucked behind her back was her left hand, while she extended her gloved right hand. "Give me that note," she whispered. "That's the last straw."

Kim placed the note in Sister Jackson's opened palm. Her large eyes glistened and started to water. "It isn't mine."

"I know, hun. I saw Sunday writing the note." She narrowed her eyes. "You should be ashamed of yourself.

Just because you're the pastor's daughter doesn't mean the same rules don't apply to you."

With Sister Jackson off her post, the double doors opened quietly. A hush fell over the church. A few of the members turned to investigate. Medium build, with long silky legs, a young Caucasian woman stood at the door. Dressed in a short black skirt, she ran her blue eyes over the congregation, as if searching for someone.

When she found *that* person, she tossed her blonde tresses, then strutted toward him. The cute guy scooted over to make room for her. She sat beside him, wiggling to get comfortable. Then, she raised his arm, and placed it around her shoulders.

At that point, I could hardly breathe. By sending him a childish note, I almost made a terrible mistake. Because the woman nuzzled her face affectionately against his, it was obvious they were an item.

It's Sunday!

Apparently, she had been in the restroom, while cutie pie found a seat. Lesson learned. Don't assume all handsome guys are unattached.

Still taunting me, Sister Jackson pointed toward the front of the church. "Sit by your mother."

Members of the church watched our commotion. They frowned, and my cheeks burned with embarrassment. "Please, Sister Jackson. I'm too old to sit near my mother. I promise, I won't do it anymore."

"I know you won't," she spewed. "Now move."

I scooted to the edge of the pew. Everyone was watching me, including the blonde.

Reluctantly, I grabbed my purse and stood up. As I made my way to the outer aisle, my father made an unexpected announcement. "We've got a solo request for Sister Sunday. Looks like she was already on her way up here."

Seeming to know my plight, the entire church laughed. Yes. I was getting into mischief.

I was caught off guard, but God is gracious. He brought a song to my memory. After taking my place in the choir stand. I walked up to the microphone; mounting tension made my steps shorter. To gather my courage, I looked at the floor. Then, I closed my eyes — taking myself before the presence of almighty God. I opened my mouth and drew in a breath. ♪"Why should I feel discouraged? And why, should the shadows— come. His eye—is on—the sparrow. And I know, he's watching over me."

A member from the guest church stood up and shouted, "Thank you Lord! Thank you Lord!" As she jumped and rejoiced, Sister Jackson rushed toward her. She fanned the woman and made sure she didn't harm herself or anyone else.

Soon, my mother leaped to her feet. "Glory, glory!" she screamed, swinging her arms. The woman seated on the front row, dodged the swift movement of her arms.

It's Sunday!

Before long, the entire church was in an uproar. There was crying, leaping and praising God.

When church was over, I learned that the interracial couple was married, and his father was the visiting pastor.

If I rode home with my dad, I'd have more time to talk to my friends. So, I waved goodbye to mother, telling her I'd catch my father home.

Preachers have several meetings after church, and this day was no exception. "Wait right here," he called, pulling off his preacher's robe. "I've gotta meet with Brother Goodman and Brother Jefferson."

It was late evening, the deacon was locking the church doors, and my friends were already gone. "But, Daddy. If I had known you were going to be this late, I would have ridden home with mama."

Daddy paused, with his jaw set. Then, as if exasperated, he rolled his eyes toward the ceiling. "But you didn't, huh? So now you're stuck with me." He draped the robe across his arm.

I folded my arms and slumped onto the first pew. "We're going to be here all night. There's no one in the kitchen. They've all gone home."

My father tilted his head to one side. "That's not my problem, now is it?" He turned and walked away.

Still a daddy's girl, I called to him. "Daddy. Daddy!" Ignoring my plea, my father disappeared behind the door of the pastor's study.

The sanctuary was quiet, and I was utterly alone. I walked to the back of the church and opened the door. There were three cars in the parking lot and the sun was slowly setting. I peered down the hallway toward the classrooms.

All of the lights were out, so I sat back down on the pew with arms folded. What on earth was I going to do for thirty minutes?

An old hymnal lay on the pew beside me. As I had done thousands of times, I fanned the pages looking for the words to a song—any song, it really didn't matter, I needed to busy myself.

It's Sunday!

The building must have been settling; a creaking noise came from the right side of the room. Though I'd heard it before, this time, it startled me. In warning, electricity darted across my shoulders, and I looked up. Once again, no one was there.

Disturbed by the eeriness of my solitude, I studied the words in the hymnal once more. Feeling cautious, I attuned my ears.

In my soul, I knew something wasn't right. I lowered the book, then tapered my eyes with suspicion. The ceiling seemed fine. Each light fixture was intact. There were no insects buzzing about them.

Then I listened. A soft humming sound came from the direction of the choir stand. I chuckled to myself. Maybe someone had forgotten to turn off the speaker system. However, that wasn't the case.

To my left, sunlight burst through the window, washing me with a brilliant and intense white light. My eyes felt uncomfortable under its luster. Immediately, I threw up my forearm to shield my sight.

The light moved slowly to the middle of the sanctuary, then it started to ascend. Lodged high in the ceiling, it wavered as gently as heat from a desert floor.

Not believing my eyes, a gasp caught in my throat. I wanted to run, yet I felt compelled to stay.

Was it the ghost I once feared haunted the old church? Was it an angel, sent by God? Whatever it was, it beckoned; drawing me into its splendor. Stricken with awe, I succumbed to the majesty of the presence.

Shafts of glowing light encompassed my entire body. A surge of energy rested upon my head, and I bowed beneath it. Suddenly it rushed over my entire body and quickened my spirit. Moved to tears, emotions arose from the pit of my stomach. I turned inside the shimmer, looking at my hands and feet.

It's Sunday!

Though blinded by its radiance, there was no fear. Now, I understood. This was a messenger of love and peace — the essence of a living God.

The light spoke directly to my spirit. I nodded and understood. No, I was not walking in my destiny. There were too many distractions in my life. And yes, I had work to do.

When the light had given its message, it dissipated, leaving a feeling of peace and tranquility.

Immediately, I knew I had stood before a mighty presence. Raising my head, I knitted my brows and searched for the rare vision. After seeing and hearing nothing, I fell to my knees. Rivers of tears erupted from my soul. Although, I touched many with my singing voice, my assignment would be much deeper than I had imagined.

After I wiped my tears, I stood and walk toward the lobby. Though the presence was gone, I felt someone was indeed with me. After placing my hand on the knob of my father's office, I turned it.

Was I moving in slow motion? I had to tell someone about this marvelous thing. Exhilarated by my experience, I pushed the door open. Excitement filled my lungs. "Daddy! Daddy!"

The deacons gawked at each other with grave expressions. Though they were discussing church business, I was positive they'd noticed my frazzled condition.

Could I have waited a few more minutes? Because I had interrupted a full-blown business meeting, I was totally embarrassed.

The men grinned. Taking in my expression, my father laughed, too. His shoulders moved beneath his humor.

"What are you doing now, Sunday?" He pushed his chair backwards and stood up.

Unashamed, I ran into the comfort of his blessed arms. Would he understand? "Daddy, I saw something. I saw something strange."

He raised his brows, lifted my chin and gazed into my terrified eyes. "What was it? A mouse. A spider. What?"

This was something I couldn't explain. "Nothing, I guess. I thought I saw someone standing by the woman's bathroom."

Apparently, the men wanted to appease me. Playing the role of champions, they got up from their seats and walked into the dark hallway. Of course, no one was there.

CHAPTER TEN
A Call to the Ministry

During my early twenties, I was often asked to render special concerts, and perform on major choir projects. Appearing in many local churches, boredom set in, and the burnout phase started. I saw the same people, sang the same songs, and went to the same places.

Yes, I was a preacher's daughter, yet there was something missing from my busy life. Like most people, I had my share of trials and tribulations. Even when times were mellow, I still witnessed a void in my life. This empty feeling would be filled, during the next phase of my life.

A gospel music concert was held at the civic center. Though it was typical, the house was full. Energy filled the air as the crowd anticipated the all-star line-up. Standing backstage, I felt more like a spectator than of a participant. Nothing stirred inside me.

It's Sunday!

While I peered from the heavy velvet curtains, I looked for my family and friends seated in the audience. Seeing them in the second row, I gave a discrete wave.

When I pulled myself to an upright position, I was startled by a woman who had slipped backstage. Her steps were lively; the dim lights highlighted the gray streaks in her black hair. She was young, and thin. Round eyes appeared sunken and desperate. I moved to the side; perhaps she was next to perform. Instead, the woman grasped my arm in desperation. Then, she gazed into my eyes.

"Sister Sunday. Do you have a second?"

Taking in her weary appearance, I nodded.

"I've heard you sing," she said, her voice frantic. "And I know you know the Lord. Will you pray for me?"

"Ah, yeah. Sure."

Her face was ashen with fatigue. The tight grip she had on my arm felt uncomfortable.

This woman needed help. Like hearing the truth from God's own lips, her words quickened my thirsty spirit. I realized it was not about making melody to God, or entertaining God. There was a mission behind the praise. I needed to feed his sheep.

"My name is Rosie Smith," she said. "I've been married for seven wonderful years — or so, I thought. This year I found out my husband had been cheating on me for six of those years. He even has two other children — a boy and a girl."

Immediately, my heart went out to Rosie. I stroked her shoulder. "Oh, my God. I'm so sorry."

"Sister Sunday. It gets worse. We have two small children of our own. Now Jesse, my husband, has had a stroke. Only thirty-four years old, and he had a massive stroke. Now, hospital bills are eating us alive. Jesse can't work. He's paralyzed on his left side."

"Oh, no."

"Don't ask me what happened to that woman he was seeing. I really don't care.

It's Sunday!

Right now, Jesse is my responsibility. He lives in my house. I can't turn my back on him. That's not God's way. He's on a walker, Sister Sunday. Now, he's having mini strokes."

Hearing the announcer calling my name, I turned my eyes toward the awaiting stage. "I'm so sorry." I pulled myself from the glare of her burdened eyes.

"Please. I know you've got to go, but I'm not finished. When I found out about this woman and those children, I wanted to divorce Jesse. Everyone knew about this woman except me. I cried for weeks, trying to understand what I did to deserve such torture."

She broke down in tears, and I embraced her. Her pain was real. The agony of it tore through my heart. Now, a young woman, I had never experienced anything so horrid.

Out front, the announcer hesitated, then nodded for me to come on stage. Behind the curtain, there was a woman in crisis. It was difficult to leave her.

"And after Miss Sunday, we will have the Harmony Singers." Apparently, nervous, the man babbled about performances in the gospel line-up for the evening. I could tell he was stalling.

God touched my heart, and a prayer erupted from my soul. *"Lord, God of heaven. I thank you for every good and perfect thing that you have given us, thus far. We come to you this day, on behalf of your child, Rosie. Lord, you made her. You know the pain she's experiencing right now. You have all power to deliver, heal, and set free. Bless her family. Heal her husband, in Jesus' name. Enlarge their territory, financially, emotionally, and spiritually. In Jesus' name, I pray, Amen."*

Rejoicing, we both touched and agreed. Rosie smiled and her face shone brightly. Her stress seemed to melt and dissipate. I knew her spirit had been renewed. We hugged each other and cried. There was no doubt, God would answer her prayer. As Rosie backed away, she removed her fingers from her trembling lips, to toss me a holy kiss.

It's Sunday!

This event was no accident. I recalled the strange vision I'd witnessed at church. God had summoned me. It wasn't about entertainment—it was much more. Then I understood. He wanted me to minister to these people—feed his sheep.

Wiping tears from my eyes, I fixed my clothes, then walked out on stage. As I walked, God placed a song on my heart. I reached for the microphone, and then ministered to the entire assembly.

"Good evening ladies and gentlemen. Some of you might be going through some difficult times in your life. No one knows why you're wearing that frown. But Glory to God—God knows.

He knows what you need, and he knows what you want. Right now, Jesus is the only one who can give you back your joy. Amen. Let's tell Jesus all about our struggles. He's the only one who can help you. Jesus and Jesus alone!" Then I opened my mouth and sang. ♪"I must tell Jesus, all of my trials. I cannot bear these burdens alone."

Before I finished my song, the Pastor jumped up and extended an invitation to discipleship.

With palms turned upwards, he pleaded, "Will You Come. God knows your desires. God knows your needs. Come to Jesus!"

People started to rise from their chairs. From the back of the room, the infirmed came forward. Mothers came with infants in their arms. The elderly came on walkers. There was a total uprising, and people cried out for God to heal them. A line of people stretched around the auditorium, each one needing a special touch from God.

Standing on stage, I watched this great multitude as they reached out to their savior. My knees, buckled beneath my weigh, and I wept.

I then realized that my thoughts needed to be in total subjection to God's will. In order to accomplish what God had me to do; I had to identify with someone that was going through.

It's Sunday!

At this time, I was young. I didn't really know what it meant to pray for others. I felt this job needed to go to a much more seasoned person—a person closer to the Lord. Who was I, but a kid with no life experience?

CHAPTER ELEVEN
Gospel Recording Artist

With the life style I was living, my parents should have named me Harmony. As the years passed, my family sang after my father finished his sermons. By the age of twenty, I took over the young adult choir as choir director. God gave me assurance that I would go further than I had ever anticipated.

Drew played bass guitar. Often, he would have jam sessions with other musicians. Not only were these sessions necessary, they were also the highlight of my day. Friends would sit in, eager to sing. Gladly, they'd add their ideas to the compositions.

My brother and his friends formed a group known as Bradford & Company. We performed at concerts, banquets, and out-door benefits. A professional saxophone player, Vernard Johnson, traveled around the world playing his instrument and sharing his testimony.

It's Sunday!

Vernard became my inspiration. Succeeding against the odds, Vernard had made it through his tragedy. Now, he reaped the benefits of reaching out to people who needed something solid to hold on to. After almost losing his vocal abilities, he made a firm commitment to God. If God would restore his voice, he would use his gift to praise him.

With Vernard's testimony locked inside my heart, I decided to contact him. I was sure he could help me pursue my singing ministry. Placing a few phone calls, I located Mr. Johnson. Soon, I was standing on his doorstep. Anticipation of a promising future caused my heart to leap inside my chest.

Dr. Johnson opened the door and grinned. In a raspy voice he said, "You must be, Sunday." He extended his hand. "It's a pleasure to meet you. Come inside."

I stepped into Mr. Johnson's dwelling. Immediately, I was swallowed up by his vast collection of rare recordings.

When Mr. Johnson had shared their history with me, we settled on the sofa to discuss my request.

"Can I get anything for you?" He placed the soda he had been drinking on the coffee table.

Enamored by his collection, I studied each decorative piece. This collection was probably something I'd never see again. "No thanks."

He slapped his knees. "Now. What can I do for you?"

"Will you help me with my singing ministry, Dr. Johnson?"

He leaned back on the sofa and placed his palms together. "Well, what exactly are you trying to do?"

I shrugged. "I want to make a recording."

Laughter erupted in his chest. "Sure, I'll help you. That should be no problem."

After placing my confidence in Dr. Johnson, I left his home with feelings of grandeur.

* * * * *

This was it! The recording was finished.

It's Sunday!

Working with a major recording studio, I felt I was finally on my way to stardom. My first single was entitled, *Struggles. Struggles* was written by Dr. Johnson. Later, he introduced me to other producers and musicians. Producer Bert Cross produced the recording, *He's Worthy*.

One glorious day, my single was going to be played on the radio. The producers informed me of the airing date, and time. On this particular show, the listening audience was free to rate the new releases.

However, everyone didn't appreciate this new voice. One lady said, "I think she's doing a lot of screaming." Another said, "I like the song. She has a nice voice. I love the way she held that note at the end. The record should do well."

Mostly people seemed to like and appreciate the words. True enough, I didn't realize the struggles I was about to encounter. Still, quite young, I had very little experience with life.

* * * * *

Only twenty-two at the time, my first debut was held in my church. I recalled being very nervous before the concert, but mostly excited. There were people in the audience from everywhere. Jerrica did my make up, and picked out my wardrobe. My flipped hairstyle accentuated my face, while the floor-length pink lace gown, gave me an elegant feel.

Waiting impatiently, I paced the dressing room. My past life swirled inside my head. I envisioned singing in the bathroom as a youth, and I recalled the school talent shows.

Then, the thought of many church congregations burst into my mind. Now, it was time to bring out what God had placed in me all those years ago—his gift of praise.

In the sanctuary, the introduction was beginning. My skin prickled at the sound of it. Musicians had started to play for my grand entrance. Background singers and a choir chimed in.

It's Sunday!

Hearing my cue, I walked down the hallway and toward the auditorium—my breath quickened.

The announcer called out, "Now! Put your hands together for Dallas' own, Sunday Stepney!"

My manager joined me in the hall. Grinning broadly, he walked in front of me. Behind him, I floated down the church aisles to the sound of thunderous applause. People were standing, smiling, whistling, and clamoring for my acknowledgement. This time, I felt like a real celebrity. I waved my hand, and the crowd went wild.

It would have been easy to take credit for the turnout. However, being a child of God, I knew who earned this credit. A pep talk rang in my head. *No matter what you see or hear, it's not about you. It's not about you. It's all about Jesus.*

Standing before the crowd, I scanned the audience and beamed. Then, I grabbed the microphone.

This was the moment I'd been waiting for. I joined the song already in progress.

♫"I don't have no doubt, that he can work it out."

Everyone was still standing. They clapped as we continued to glorify God. The concert was long, but seemingly, the people enjoyed every minute. My first concert was the most memorable. To God be the glory.

When the crowd abated, I stood in the foyer of the church, bidding everyone goodbye, and thanking them for coming.

Like any proud sister, Jerrica flitted around me. "Girl, you tore those songs up!"

I blushed, but didn't reply. The evening had been emotional. My vision was not clear, and my contacts felt uncomfortable. With a down-turned face, I stroked my eyelids vigorously.

A man wearing a neatly pressed suit stood before me, thus obstructing my view. Annoyed, I glanced upward. "Shawn. Shawn Davis?"

Immediately, Shawn raised a brow. He held a delicate pink rose tied with frilly streams of pink ribbon. "Sunday." Leaning forward, he kissed my cheek.

It's Sunday!

His fragrant cologne adhered to my skin. "You were awesome tonight. I'm really proud of you."

"Oh my goodness, Shawn. Look at you. You're all grown up. I had no idea you were here. Thank you so much for coming. You heard about the concert, huh?"

Shawn hesitated. He looked at the pink rose, then gave it to me. "I wouldn't have missed this for the world."

"Thank you. The rose is beautiful. It's so thoughtful." Taking Shawn's arm, I moved him to the side of the foyer. Musicians were loading their instruments and we were standing in the way. "Tell me." I marveled at his well-groomed appearance. "What have you been up to?"

"Well." Shawn ran his fingers through his curly hair. "A little bit of this and a little bit of that. Right now, I'm pulling together a concert for March and April. It will be held at my church. You interested?"

Singing at Shawn's church would be an honor. "Really?"

"Yeah, check your calendar. See if you can fit us into your busy schedule."

Surprised Shawn came to show his support, a case of nerves tumbled inside my stomach. "You know I don't have a calendar for next year. Yet. But, it's so good to see you again. You look great."

We walked outside the building and toward the parking lot. People continued to pat my back with congratulations. Engulfed in Shawn's presence, I barely noticed them.

Finally, Shawn stopped walking. "You know, we never finished that project we started. Why don't we finish it tomorrow night? It shouldn't take long."

I was honored. After all these years, Shawn had found no one to finish the project. Naturally, I hadn't heard from him. I assumed Lisa had finished the track. Mystified, by his confession I felt confusion resting on my brow. "I can't believe you never finished that project."

As if embarrassed, Shawn hung his head. "No." He shuffled his foot against the concrete. His dress shoes gleamed against oncoming headlights.

It's Sunday!

"I couldn't. No one else could capture the emotions of that song like you. I know I was young at the time, but I had enough business sense not to settle for less. So, I placed the project on hold until I could find you again."

"Tell me you're joking."

"No." He shook his head. "I wish I could." Shawn pulled back his suit coat, then shoved his hands into his pockets. "How about tomorrow morning?"

I had a radio interview the next day, with KGGX Gospel Radio. Nevertheless, I really didn't want to lose contact with him, ever again. "You know—I have a radio interview in the morning. I need a ride, would you be willing to pick me up?"

A wide grin spread across his face. "I'd love to pick you up. We could set up some things for my upcoming project."

* * * * *

The next morning, Shawn picked me up at 5:00 a.m. The broadcast was scheduled to air at 6:00 a.m. Uneasy with my task, perspiration beaded across my breasts.

I had no idea what the radio announcer would ask. During the interview, I watched Shawn from across the room. His pleasant expression made me feel more relaxed, and at ease. Therefore, the interview was a big success.

Afterwards, I walked outside the door with a childish giggle. "Boy. I'm glad that's over."

Shawn ran his hand across my shoulder. "Good job, kid. Why don't we go somewhere for breakfast and talk for a while."

We had much to talk about. "Sure," I nodded. "I'd like that."

Breakfast was Shawn's treat. Before our breakfast arrived, Shawn made a startling confession. "Sunday. I'm going to stop the lies. I'm interested in you."

Hearing his words, a lump arose in my throat. I picked up my glass of water and took a swallow. "Ah, okay."

"I have no idea how you feel about me." As if waiting for my reply, he cocked his head to one side.

It's Sunday!

I nodded, and pulled my silver from my napkin. My insides were screaming, *Yes!*

Gazing into my eyes Shawn admitted, "We both have busy schedules — with our music and all."

"That's true."

"Well. Do you think we could move our friendship to the next level?"

For years, I had longed for this conversation to take place. In my heart, I felt this was *not* our time. With demanding schedules, it would be difficult to engage in a committed relationship. Speechless, I returned Shawn's gaze.

"I like you very much, Shawn. But, it would be difficult to engage in a committed relationship. We're just starting our careers. Maybe another day, and another time, we'll meet again. Perhaps the terms will be different. I'm so sorry."

Shawn looked down at his breakfast, then shook his head. "Are you sure, Sunday? I mean we haven't even tr…"

Before Shawn could finish, I was shaking my head. "It's not good for us."

He sighed and pushed his meal aside. "I've wasted my time, huh?"

I placed my hand on his arm, and caressed it. "I wouldn't say that. We've had a great time."

"Well," Shawn narrowed his eyes, "is it possible to ask one thing of you — before I walk out of your life?"

"Sure." Disappointed with my own decision, I shrugged. "What is it?"

He stroked his chin thoughtfully, then averted his eyes. "I've always wondered what your kisses were like. Would you grant me that honor? We may never meet again."

My cheeks reddened, but I agreed.

During the ride home, Shawn was quiet. When we arrived at my house, he leaned toward me, and pulled me into his arms. "Sunday," he whispered, brushing his lips across mine. Without hesitation, he sought the sweetness inside.

Beneath his spell, I closed my eyes. The fevers of his passion jolted my body to a heightened state.

It's Sunday!

Shocked at my body's response, I widened my eyes, then I pushed him away. Mixed emotions churned, leaving me breathless, yet disappointed.

I had satisfied my curiosity, and I loved every minute in his fragrant arms. When I reached for the door's handle, Shawn rested his hand on the steering wheel.

As if deep in thought, he stared straight ahead. Then, he faced me with raised brows. "Sunday."

The door swung open. Hearing my name, I glanced over my shoulder. "Yes."

His eyes glistened; he touched his lips. "Sunday. Are you really sure?" he pressed.

I sighed and reached for my purse. Was I going to regret this decision? It was hardly fair to string him along. "Yes, Shawn. I'm sure."

I closed the door, and then walked toward my home. Why did I feel so empty inside?

CHAPTER TWELVE
A Night to Remember

Almost overnight, I became a singing sensation. I did concerts, and appeared with major recording artists. Fans even asked for my autograph. Performing for major stage plays and after parties, was enough to keep my mind and thoughts moving in the right direction. I was privileged enough to open for a widely-known gospel group — The *Winans.* This event was a night, I'd never forget. The concert was held at the city's best location; the Dallas Convention Center. The world's most popular talent had performed there. We were given posh dressing rooms, with bright, lighted mirrors. While we waited to go on, there were trays of food, fruit, and iced beverages

One of the program's announcers came to the door to inform us, "You have ten minutes before you're on."

While I waited, I prayed, meditated, and tried to prepare myself. My sister donned me in gown and make-up.

It's Sunday!

This was all I ever dreamed about as a child. Being a Gospel Recording Artist, and performing on stage with celebrities. This was surreal. My opportunity to make a lasting impression had arrived.

Background singers, musicians, and everyone prepared to go on stage. I ran out of the dressing room, through the convention's large kitchen area, then down a long hallway. The massive auditorium was my goal. Then, there it was—a stage grander than anything I'd ever known. The program announcer's voice rang out loud and clear. "And now, please welcome to the stage, one of Dallas' own, Gospel Recording Artists, Sunday Stepney and Friends."

As we ran closer to the stage, I saw all nationalities. Young and old were staring as we ran down the aisle. My heart was beating loudly. Seconds felt like minutes. Seemed it took forever to get to on stage.

A middle-aged man took my arm to assist me up the stairs and to the stage area. I took my position, and looked at the audience.

People directly in front of me were visible, but the crowd was hidden behind bright lights. A huge spotlight shined directly into my eyes. At that time, I made a decision to focus my attention on something else.

I took a deep breath; and ministered to the people I could see. With this in mind, I would treat them as if they were the only ones in the room—a small crowd.

As musicians and background vocals took their places behind me, I finally spoke to the crowd, to get over my fear.

I said, "How's everybody doing out there? Has God done anything for you? Is he worthy to be praised? Come on, put your hands together."

The music started. I had four keyboard players, a lead guitarist, a bass player and about six to eight background singers. Almost every musician in Dallas wanted to play in this event for me. It was an honor to open for the *Winans*.

It's Sunday!

The background singers began to sing. ♫"You are worthy, blessed savior, we will crown you lord of all, halleluiah, glory to your name, he's great and holy, worthy to be praised."

Immediately, I came in, ♫"He's worthy to be praised."

The music was loud. All I could see was people standing, clapping, and witnessing. Everything seemed to move in fast motion. Before long, I found myself at the end of the song.

The background sang, ♫ "Worthy to be praised."

And, I repeated, ♫"Worthy to be praised." Then, I sustained the note in a high-pitched soprano voice.

The music continued as the announcer entered the stage again. "Put your hands together again, for Sister Sunday Stepney." As we left the stage, people cheered and clapped.

Because I'm very clumsy, I tried to stay on my feet. People patted us on the back with enthusiasm. "Good job," they said, "that was really good."

* * * * *

As fate would have it, we performed at the Dallas Fair Park. This stage was outside and there was no audience. "Sing!" the man who booked our group demanded. "Just start singing, someone will come and listen. Go ahead. Start singing."

Well, I decided to act as if it was just a rehearsal. True enough, people walked up, sat in the audience, and listened. The feeling was exhilarating. Excellent music, a wonderful melody, and the heart of the song, had drawn the crowd's attention. All for the glory of God. Praise him.

* * * * *

Visiting the local radio stations kept my mind occupied. I enjoyed hanging out, and going to interviews, although they generally took place before daylight. Though inconvenient, it was well worth the trouble. During these interviews, the radio announcers would play our singles, and then allow listeners to call in, and chat.

It's Sunday!

Generally, the public was pretty nice. From time to time, we'd have rude callers who'd hide behind the cover of the airways, with insults. The radio announcers always gave us good feedback, and sound advice for marketing, promotion, and managing. Anytime they sponsored an event, they'd ask us to perform.

I made new friends and kept my old ones. God has a way of placing special people in your path. Flamboyant, seasoned, and honest, Wanda Merrit was one of those people.

Wanda and I recorded singles around the same time. Sometimes, we were even on the same radio programs. After a set, we'd usually get a bite to eat. I wasn't sure about eating breakfast at this new restaurant; however, Wanda assured me, the food was superb. We sat in a booth, shoveled food into our mouths, and behaved like wild teens.

Wanda took a sip from her coffee, then pointed her designer nails in my direction. "No, no, no, my friend.

The short bald one is yours, and the Jeri-curl is mine."

Munching bacon, I leaned back in my seat. "You've got to be kidding. He's old as dirt."

"Yeah, but he's kinda cute." Wanda loved hair fashions; she pushed a bleached blonde curl from her face. "Just look at that face." She pursed her full lips to stifle her laughter. "You're a lot younger than I am, Sunday. That's why people like your singing better."

A server dropped a cup and I turned in response. "People like all kinds of music, Wanda. My style is just different." I raked a small portion of eggs on my toast. "I don't believe a word you're saying."

"I hear you," Wanda warned, adding syrup to her pancakes. "But, you need to put yourself out there. Sell yourself, girl. Toot your own horn. Remember the autograph signing session, when the other artists flew in. We took full advantage of those sessions. Didn't we?"

It's Sunday!

"Yeah. We did. Being a part of National Recording Artist does make me feel important."

"Honey, you can't be shy. You're a recording artist now. Act like it! Stop sittin' in the back row of them auditoriums. Do like me. Remember what I told that guy?" She cocked her head to one side. "Okay, Wanda is here now, baby. Direct me to the front. You've gotta feel the success. Stop sitting on that back row waiting for success to fall in your lap."

"But, Wanda. I'm kinda laid back, and a little shy and bashful."

She raised her fork to her lips, but stopped. "Girl. You've gotta say, Excuse me! I'm Sunday Stepney. Ya'll step aside. That's right, step aside."

Wanda was animated, and always made me laugh. "Yeah, I remember. You told them, *we were both* recording artists, then asked them if they wanted *your* autograph?"

We burst into laughter as we recalled the comical incident.

"Darn right. It's a dog eat dog world, Sunday. There's no room for a toy poodle. Girl. You've gotta be a bulldog." Wanda flexed her feminine muscles.

Wanda was street smart, but she was really a God fearing woman. She was trying desperately to teach me how to honor the ministry. I learned a lot from Wanda, and her no fear attitude. Reason, season, I always say. People come into your life for a reason, or a season. There were always lessons to be learned.

It's Sunday!

CHAPTER THIRTEEN
Wife and Mother

By age twenty-three, my schedule was so tight, I had no time to meet or date guys. On New Year's Eve, a curious prank caller put my life into a tailspin that would eventually change my life.

Everyone was getting into the holiday spirit, but I wasn't feeling it. I watched television programs to herald in the New Year. After talking with my large family all evening, I decided to take a break. Then, the phone rang once more.

"Hello."

"Hi," a masculine voice replied. "Is this Sunday?"

"Yes. This is Sunday. How may I help you?"

"You're kidding me, right? I mean, like, no one is named Sunday."

Good thing I had a sense of humor about my name. "Yes. I know."

"I found your name in my friend's black book. I thought you were some prayer line or something."

"Well, that's original. No, it's just me, Sunday."

The caller's voice was very romantic, and for some strange reason I hung on his every word. Was I desperate, or just stupid? After talking until New Year's day, we learned a lot about each other. We were both into music. He played several instruments. Was it fate? Was it God's divine will?

When we discovered he had attended my father's church, I cringed. It's funny how fate has a way of taking you out of a person's life, until you're ready to receive what God has for you. Anyway, I was thrilled. I informed my family about the small miracle. This man was going to be special, and I knew it.

It was time to end the game by meeting my mystery man. I instructed him to meet me at my cousin's house. Then, I asked my cousin, Taylor, to answer the door when he arrived.

"Okay," she said, with a devilish grin. "I'll open the door. If he's a dog, I'll tell him you left. If he's cute, I'll come to the den and give you the signal."

It's Sunday!

"I'm so nervous. I've been on blind dates before, but there is something about this guy that spooks me."

Taylor placed her hand on her hips. "You said he sounded like a nice guy."

"I know, but voices can be deceiving."

She looked down at my clothing and sighed. "Please tell me you're not wearing that?"

I shrugged. "What's wrong with what I'm wearing?"

"Sunday." She rolled her eyes. "A tee shirt and leggings? Really?"

"Hey. I'm comfortable, alright?"

"No. You're a geek—man repellent. What's up with the glasses? Where are your contacts?"

"I want him to see me like I really am." I smirked. "No airs. Then I'll know for sure."

"Suit yourself." Taylor turned up her nose, then walked away. "He's here anyway. There's no time to change."

A knock on the door, and I ran into the den and listened.

From there I could hear everything happening out front. Would he be a cutie or would he be dog ugly?

Taylor walked back to the den. She was grinning so hard I thought her face would crack. "He's a doll."

"Don't trick me, girl. I'll kick your butt if you're lying to me." I stretched my eyes toward the living room to get a peek. All I saw was his back and a neatly combed Jeri curl. I felt my own Jeri curl, then looked down at my sneakers. I didn't exactly look like the greatest catch. "Okay, Taylor. I'm coming."

From that date, we clicked like pieces to a puzzle. There were more dates to come. We both loved music and tennis. Basically, we fell heads over heels in love. My next move was taking him to church.

Being a drummer, guitarist, and percussionist could benefit both our careers. However, Gerald's thing was jazz. Even so, daddy welcomed him to the church, and encouraged him to use his talents to enhance church services.

It's Sunday!

Though jazz ran deep in his veins, Gerald appeared to love the role he played in the church. Because we were both into music, I became comfortable in his company. We spent time going to the movies and dinner. Often, we dressed alike to take pictures, and went to the park.

Church was my life and soon, Gerald became a part of it. After a year, we considered a lifetime commitment. Plans for marriage, entered our conversation.

With that promise, the pressures of intimacy arrived. Stealing private moments at his parents' house had repercussions. Engagement was not a marriage license. Nevertheless, we were over twenty, and treated it as such.

Protection would be necessary as we both felt we were responsible young adults. After our encounter, we continued to date. But, guilt consumed me. All I could think about was being out of God's will. An impending fear loomed in my mind, day and night. I had allowed a man to become the object of my desire.

Then, one day, the moment of truth arrived. I sat in church feeling dizzy and light-headed. My father preached out of his soul, yet his voice seemed to waver in and out. Perspiration beaded on my forehead.

"What's wrong?" Jaden asked, stroking my back.

"I don't know." I blotted my face with a torn tissue, while my stomach lurched uneasily. "I feel faint. I think I have a virus."

"Didn't you eat anything for breakfast?"

"Don't say breakfast," I whispered. "Just the smell of bacon makes me sick." Holding my stomach, I leaned forward and wretched.

"You look terrible," she uttered softly. "Go to the restroom and freshen up."

"I'm not sure I can make it." I stood to my feet, took two steps, then, emptied my stomach onto the carpeted floor. The next thing I knew, someone was helping me outside and into the fresh air.

My mother rushed to be by my side. Another woman left the sanctuary to assist her. I sat on the steps trying to catch my breath while the world around me spun out of control.

"Is she alright?" the woman asked, addressing my mother.

"Yeah." Mother nodded. "She's going to be okay. She's just pregnant."

Horrors. My mother felt I was pregnant. I looked into her stern face, tears welling up inside me. "Mama. Is that true?"

Mama placed her hand around my shoulders. "Yes. It's not a virus, honey. But, it's going to be alright." She rocked me in her arms and stroked my hair.

"I'm so sorry, Mama. I've disappointed you. We were trying to be careful."

"Sweetie." Mama pulled my torrid face toward hers. She wiped my tears with a gentle sweep of her thumb. "Sometimes careful isn't good enough. It's called abstinence."

Mother was right. Yes, I was pregnant, two months to be exact.

Now, damaged goods, I would become a reluctant bride. God was unable to use me. That thought took an emotional toll. Conflict took the joy out of marriage.

* * * * *

December 10, 1988, was a cold and rainy night. Somehow, the dismal weather dimmed the festive mood of the wedding. Had the weather foretold the outcome of my marriage? Two clueless people were trying desperately to make things right in the sight of God. Hopefully, God would bless our commitment, and honor our union.

Jerrica was my Matron of Honor. Knowing my heart, as sisters do, she helped me into my gown, while spurring a smile from my worried expression.

"Come on Sunday. Smile. This is your day."

"I don't know, Jerrica." I cast my eyes toward the floor. "This is not how I pictured my life."

"Okay. So, it's your special day. And, you're going to walk around being miserable?"

"No." I wiped a forming tear.

"Sunday." She pointed toward the sanctuary. "There is a handsome man out there waiting for you." Placing her flowers aside, she then secured my veil. "That man loves you. Don't sit here making yourself unhappy."

"I can't help it," I groaned.

My older sister lifted my face. Our gazes met. "Sunday. Your marriage will work if you let it. Make it work."

I studied the sincerity in Jerrica's large brown eyes. Then I stood up, and pulled my train behind me. "I'm so scared. I feel like I want to run."

"If you run, I swear, I'll hit you in the back of the head with my bouquet."

Picturing Jerrica tossing her bouquet at my head, I grinned.

Jerrica pulled the veil over my face. "See. It's all good. Now, let's go."

While the music played the photographer took pictures of us in the foyer. My father waited with extended arm. "Are you ready," he asked, his eyes calm and reassuring.

I picked up the hem of my dress, interlocked my arm with his, then nodded. "Yes, Daddy."

Family and friends stood when we entered the room. They were smiling brightly as I glided down the aisle. Singing had taught me how to work a crowd, so I returned their excited smiles.

When I finally reached my husband, he stared at me from the corner of his eye. His lips were drawn so tight, they were almost a faint grimace. Was he having the same thoughts?

The church was decorated in my chosen colors of red and white—the moment was beautiful, yet surreal. Having a dutiful expression, Gerald didn't smile when he saw his bride to be.

When he took my hand, there were no bells, or whistles, nor I did I hear the melodic sound of angels singing.

Fortunately, the wedding went as planned. For some reason, the minister could barely remember, or pronounce my fiancées name.

As nervous as we both were, we knew we were doing the right thing.

It's Sunday!

The minister finally announced, "Gerald Lewis, you may now kiss your bride. With no hesitation, Gerald came toward me. The kiss lasted a second — was that also a precursor to my marriage? Right away, the wedding party and guests burst into laughter. Was this the passionate kiss they were waiting for? Gerald, a very private person, had decided not to make a spectacle of the moment. As his new bride, I had to agree.

After the wedding festivities were finally over, our honeymoon took place in an apartment my father provided as a gift. We settled into our new home, and the matrimony race commenced.

The moment I became Mrs. Gerald Lewis, I placed my singing career on hold. Mentally, my decision had dire consequences, as I longed to sing.

* * * * *

When Gerald and I were dating, Gerald had given me a beautiful doll. I named her Tuesday. One Monday, July 24th, 1989, Tuesday Lewis, a living doll, became our reality.

Tuesday's birth brought our families together with cheers of congratulations. Everyone admired the seven pound, eight ounce, baby girl. She was perfect in every way — her father made over.

Once again, our lives changed. Gerald, was an admirable father and attentive to his daughter's needs. Everyone was helpful with little Tuesday, and willing to extend their assistance, as we both worked.

However, as Tuesday's mother, I had no desire to leave my precious baby to accept singing engagements.

Because I was emotionally and physically drained, I didn't mind placing my dreams on hold. I worked as a clerk in a hospital, while Gerald's occupation was a barber. With his flexible hours, Gerald often took Tuesday to work with him.

With the passing of time, my son, Nigel, was born. Nigel, was the answer to my prayer as I also wanted a son. Soon, I lost sight of ever having a singing career.

If I didn't fulfill my destiny, perhaps my children would.

It's Sunday!

God doesn't make mistakes. People do. If God leads us, our mistakes can become our blessings.

Although, my husband and I worked faithfully in the church, confusion occurred between us. Just when I thought, everything was going good—que Satan—the destroyer of relationships, homes, churches, jobs and schools.

The tape ministry was my husband's job. His responsibility was to record Sunday morning services. Miscommunication within the church brought confusion and contention.

Numerous arguments sparked. To avoid further conflict, Gerald decided he would discontinue worshipping with his family. It was my desire that the entire family attend church together. As they say, *A family that prays together stays together.*

*****

Gerald's decision sowed discord in our marriage, and our children suffered. All things work together for good, for those who love the Lord.

Sunday Stepney Lewis

Despite my belief in God, the foundation of my marriage began to crumble. Thereafter, we started to blame each other for our unhappiness and emptiness. God is not the author of confusion.

Couples were getting divorced in droves. Knowing the answer in my heart, I questioned if *I* had put this marriage together, instead of God. Was this the man God intended *me* to marry?

The word of God is the most effective when it comes to successful relationships. We received counseling from ministers and doctors, but to no avail. Both must claim responsibility of the marriage, and both parties must be willing to let God's methods work.

As a result, sometimes counseling worked, and other times, it didn't. I moved in with my parents, and made several attempts to save my marriage. My motto was, *Nothing beats a failure but a try*.

* * * * *

Friday night was family night in my house.

It's Sunday!

Gerald would show off his culinary talents, and we became the perfect family. Nachos and punch was our family's favorite snack, and Gerald was happy to please his offspring.

Seeing his dad walk into the living room, Nigel bounced on the sofa. "Dad!" he called, pointing to the television screen. "You see that game? That's the one I want for Christmas."

Gerald placed the snacks he was carrying on the coffee table, then looking at the television screen, he grimaced. "Son. Son. Where is the last game you asked for?"

Nigel averted his eyes from his father's condemning gaze. "I don't know."

"Man it's laying around on the floor somewhere." He sat beside his son on the sofa.

Tuesday sat on the EZ chair with one leg tucked beneath her. She was not about to remain quiet. "He broke it daddy. Don't buy him nuttin'."

Nigel shrugged and gave her a look. "You shut up!

At least I don't have a virus on my computer. You downloaded a virus on your computer. Going to all them websites daddy told you not to visit."

Tuesday's scowl let Gerald know, she'd been naughty. With narrowed eyes, she drew her lips tightly. "Dumb ten year old. You tell everything you know."

"Tuesday," Gerald reprimanded, reaching for his drink. "Not again."

"Daddy," she pleaded, "it was an accident." She placed her cell phone on the arm of the chair.

Nigel leaned forward. Gloating in victory, he stuck out his tongue at Tuesday. "…told you, I was gonna get you back."

"Alright, son. That's enough." Gerald turned toward his daughter. "Tuesday, I'm not going to fix your computer until you learn to be more responsible. And Nigel, I saw that game laying on the floor. It was out of the case, man."

"Aw, man." Nigel cast his gaze toward the floor. "I didn't mean to leave it out. I was coming back."

It's Sunday!

Gerald placed his arm on the back of the sofa and crossed his legs. "You don't take pride in your games when you don't have to pay for them." He scratched his head. "I give you money every week, man. If you want that game, then save your money."

Disappointment rested on Nigel's face. "Yes, sir." He turned just in time to see Tuesday sticking out her tongue. "Dad!"

"Look," Tuesday called, pointing to the television. "The movie is on."

Gerald looked over his shoulder. "Is your mother still on the phone?"

"I'm standing right here," I said, with arms folded. "I've been listening this entire time. Nigel, your dad is teaching you to be a good steward of your money. You'd better listen, son."

The movie blasted onto the screen, but Nigel was unhappy. He huffed. "Why I gotta be a good steward of my money when Tuesday spends money like water going down a drain? It's not fair!"

After Gerald placed his drink on the coffee table, he leaned toward Nigel. "I know how to stop this mess." He tickled Nigel until he rolled over the sofa in laugher. Clearly, his kicks and screams disturbed his older sister. "No. Dad! Stop! The movie's on!"

Tuesday grabbed the remote control and turned up the volume. "Will ya'll stop wrestling. I can't hear."

Gerald turned toward his daughter. He made a claw with his fingers. "You want some of this?" he replied, with a devilish grin.

"Daddy, I'm too old for that baby stuff." Tuesday rolled her eyes. "Shh, Norbit is on."

CHAPTER FOURTEEN
Family Battle with Cancer

When I was thirty, we discovered my dad had been diagnosed with Melanoma. His illness was no surprise to him, although, his sermons reflected his concerns. Sermon after sermon, daddy preached about going to a place where the wicked shall cease from trouble and the weary shall be at rest.

Dad lived a free spirited life-style. His sermons always started with the statement. *I'm happy*. I believe that despite his illness my father felt he would be all right. To be absent from the body, is to be present with the Lord. My daddy didn't show signs of weakness, and never neglected his pastoral duties.

Periodically, he'd fall asleep on the living room sofa while watching Gun Smoke.

However, on this particular Sunday morning, dad relinquished his strength to the power of his weakened body.

Worship Services had been wonderful.

Jaden and I were in a hurry to leave, as we had a singing engagement at another church.

The car was packed with chattering women. We sped down the highway discussing what we were going to sing. Suddenly, my cell phone vibrated in my purse. I unzipped my purse, snatched up the phone and looked at the number. "It's Drew. Hope we didn't forget anything."

Jaden's eyes grew large, then narrowed into a frown. "I hope daddy is okay."

"What's up Drew?"

"Sunday. It's daddy. He collapsed in the sanctuary after services. We've called an ambulance, but the church is in an uproar."

"Really? We'll be right there." I gave the phone to Jaden, and then turned the car around in the middle of the street.

"Drew," Jaden asked, "What's happening?"

"I don't know," Drew admitted, through the phone. "He's sitting up now. But I'm worried."

It's Sunday!

"Don't worry. We're only a few miles away. We'll be right there."

When we got to the church, dad was sitting up in his chair. Because his family rallied around him, daddy wanted to know what the fuss was about. "I'm just fine." He smiled, and then mopped his forehead with his handkerchief. "I'll go to the doctor tomorrow."

In warning, I gave dad an evil eye. "Daddy."

"Don't look at me like that. I promise I'll go." He stroked my shoulder to reassure me. "You girls are supposed to be gone by now. You're gonna be late. Ya'll worry too much."

Daddy was right, we were worried sick. Leaving our hearts with our father, we went on to our singing engagement. This was the first of many battles to come.

Dad's condition had gotten worse. Weeks later, he complained of shortness of breath. He was rushed to the hospital, immediately. The physician placed a tracheal tube in his esophagus; the cancer was spreading.

Nevertheless, my father continued to speak to his congregation on Sundays, but his preaching was limited. Being a strong man, he would not let his illness hinder him from preaching the word of God.

Personally, I was in denial and questioned God. How could a merciful God allow so much distress? I wanted him to heal my daddy. God had prepared us by conditioning our minds to deal with the worst. We accepted whatever came.

Years earlier, I had dreamed of my father's death. In this dream, doctors called the family to my father's bedside to give us the bad news. While my father lay there, I recalled that my heart was saddened by the news. Awaken by the tragedy, I thrashed in bed and sobbed uncontrollably.

This dream couldn't possibly come true, right? Was it God's way of preparing me for my dad's departure?

Months later, dad requested pictures from his childhood.

With a sense of duty, he made his own funeral arrangements and gathered information for the program.

Eventually, father was placed on Hospice. On October 2nd, of 1998, I sat behind my desk. With remote actions, I picked up the same memo only to put it down, and pick it up again.

Unable to focus, I wasn't sure if I had read it or not. There was uneasiness in my spirit and concentrating was near impossible.

Then, my phone rang, almost scaring me to death. As I picked up the phone, my heart raced. "Sunday Lewis. May I help you?"

There was silence, then I heard my mother's lament. "Sunday. Your dad is gone."

Hearing the news, I closed my eyes, shook my head, and groaned. "Mama. My God." Fighting back tears, I lifted my eyes upward. "I felt this in my spirit."

"Yeah. Jerrica is taking it kinda hard."

"I knew she would. Who's with her?"

"Jaden, Jonas, and Drew are here."

I sighed, and reached for the tissue box sitting on my desk. "I guess he finished the work God had for him to do."

A whimper erupted from the phone. "Yes, he did."

"Cancer had ravaged his body." Tears ran down my cheeks. "Now, his pain and suffering is over." With reality setting in, I hesitated, then shook my head once more. "Rest in peace, daddy."

"Sunday, are you going to be okay?"

"Yes, Mama." I sniffled softly. "I guess I'd better call Gerald. The kids are going to throw a fit."

"I know, honey. But, everyone knew this was coming."

"Yeah." I paused. "But, when it actually happens, no one can say how they'll react."

Dad's services were like none other. The day of his funeral, we agreed to dress in white apparel. White was symbolic of the pure and joyous life my father tried to live. The services were indeed a home going celebration. We cried and sang praises all at the same time.

It's Sunday!

In my father's memory, my entire family sang a special song. Twenty or more family members, including in-laws, nieces, and nephews, gathered to make this event a reality.

I led the song. My sister, Jaden, came in with her high-pitched soprano voice. Suddenly, she started crying, jumping, and twitching her shoulders in her usual way. People were amazed by the strength God had given our family.

Sunday morning, worship services continued as usual. My father would have wanted it that way.

* * * * *

Trent, my elder brother, carried on my father's legacy as pastor of the church. He was voted as pastor, by the majority. It was Trent, who took the church to the next level. Because he spent a lot of time with my father, as assistant pastor, he knew the ministry's guidelines and bi-laws.

Trent's personality was quite different. Though the members complained, he was a somber man, with a limited sense of humor.

However, at home, Trent was quite the opposite. During my childhood, he made up a song about me. He called me, *Sun Stank, Lou, Lou*. Often, Trent would call and bore me with technical conversation. At church, his motto was, God is good all the time, and all the time God is good.

The church had one year under Trent's leadership, before he was also diagnosed with cancer. A small man with big ambitions would soon leave his flock. My father had organized the church. Trent made it his goal to pay off that note.

Much like my father, through his illness, he exemplified humility. In spite of his illness; under his leadership, half of the note was paid off.

This gesture humbled the entire church, but it was not enough to prevent some disgruntle members from leaving.

* * * * *

It's Sunday!

When Trent was unable to carry out his responsibilities, he passed the torch to my younger brother, Jonas, who God had also prepared. This change was very difficult for my mother as well as the entire family. The loss of my father to cancer was still fresh in our minds. My brother's family was strong, and his wife gained courage from God. In November of 2004, God called Trent home. Once again, my family had to lean on God's strength.

CHAPTER FIFTEEN
Passing the Torch

With some controversy, my brother, Jonas carried on church services. Our motives were to stand together; focusing on our faith in God.

Enthralled by God's word, I'd sit in church, held captive my brother's unique preaching style. We were closer in age, and often played together as children. While the choir sang, I watched Jonas as he nodded his head and raised his hand in praises to God.

While I watched my brother, the music seemed to fade into the distance. Remembering our childhood, a soft chortle caught in my throat. Though I was only eleven, I had a deep interest in gospel music. "When I grow up," I crowed. "I'm going to be a choir director." I turned my attention back to the choir singing on a local television show.

It's Sunday!

Jonas jumped up from the sofa. "And, I'm gonna be your pastor. Praise God! Glory Hallelujah! Bless his wonderful name!"

"Ooo! You sound just like daddy." I'd shove him playfully. We loved to play church. Could God have been preparing us, even then?

In elementary school, Jonas was protective of me. He never wanted me to wait alone when school was out. After school, we'd wait for our ride in a special place. A lush oak tree provided our shade. Recalling the cracked sidewalk, and the soothing aroma of the old tree, bittersweet memories crept through my mind.

One spring evening, ants had crawled up my pants, and tore me up. Because we were standing outside, there was not much we could do about my misery. Getting naked had not been an option. Cars rolled slowly past. Parents stopped to pick up waiting children.

"Jonas," I whined. "I'm tired of standing by this tree. These ants are eating me up!

I'm going across the street to talk to my friends."

Jonas made a fist. "Girl. You'd better not leave me, alone. Mama is gonna get mad if you're not standing by this tree."

"I don't care," I blasted, while scratching my leg. "I'm tired of these stinky old ants."

"Don't leave, Sunday." Jonas shifted the weight of his backpack, and hoisted it across his back. He widened his eyes to look down the street. "I'm gonna tell mama!" Though Jonas acted as if he was my father, he was always looking out for his baby sister.

The choir finished their song, and my daydreaming ended. Once again, I regarded Jonas sitting in daddy's regal chair. With eyes closed, he nodded his head in memory of the lively gospel music. Did I ever think Jonas would really be my pastor? Feeling melancholy, my mind took flight —back to our teen years.

It's Sunday!

Lunch was my favorite subject. Unfortunately, it was also the time weirdoes pushed their luck with unwanted flirting. This day, Reggie sat down beside me in the cafeteria. He was buff — an unusually muscular senior, and captain of the football team. For some reason, he decided I would be easy prey for his unwanted advances.

I picked up the cold sliver of pizza from my tray, then took a hearty bite. Watching Reggie from the corner of my eye, I chewed the gummy dough.

Reggie looked down at me with tapered eyes. He jutted his head forward. "Sup?"

Still chewing, I looked over my glasses to give Reggie a sidelong glance. Was he talking to me? I knew better. He was dating Gayla, the head cheerleader. A senior, Reggie was out of my league. Was it open season on freshmen that day? Not trusting his physical closeness, I watched him slyly. Beneath the table, I noticed that Reggie kept stroking his thigh.

There was an uneasy feel about him. He moistened his lips. "What? You can't speak?"

I pushed my glasses back on my nose. "I said, hey."

Reggie turned his large eyes to watch the cafeteria door; then his gaze panned the entire area. Interested in his motives, I mirrored his gaze. For some reason, the teacher's whereabouts seemed to concern him. He bit his bottom lip, then looked over his shoulder. Reggie appeared nervous. I knew he was up to mischief, I'd seen that look before.

Though Reggie was dating Gayla, he wouldn't miss an opportunity to feel up any female in close proximity. Today was no exception.

Suddenly, Reggie shoved a warm hand up my skirt. Shocked, I widened my eyes. "Stop boy! Don't do that!" Why was I trying to be discrete? I was the one being violated.

From across the cafeteria my brother must have heard my cry of distress. Moving with quick steps, Jonas pushed himself between us.

It's Sunday!

"Leave her alone, man." Only a sophomore, Jonas was small for his age. I was sure he shook in his pants. Like David to Goliath, God had given him boldness and courage.

Reggie gawked at Jonas. He grimaced, then slowly removed his hand from my thigh. "Hey, man," he said, as he stroked his chin. "I was just playing." Pushing his chair aside, Reggie then stood up, and towered above Jonas.

Jonas was nose to navel with Reggie's large frame. Even so, Jonas continued to bluff Reggie with an inflated chest and a horrid scowl. As in times past, it was clear Jonas was my hero.

Apparently giving up, Reggie raised both hands. "Alright, little dude. It's cool."

Jonas' lips were drawn tight. He was breathing hard. Anyone could see it would not be a fair fight. Where were the teachers when you needed one?

God had conditioned my brother to stand up for his little sister, although he was generally shy and quiet.

In a crisis, Jonas's love for his sister always came beaming through.

Who would have thought that one day, Jonas would become my spiritual father? From birth, our lives were predestined according to God's will. In order to fulfill that destiny we would need to stay on track. Unfortunate for us, our lives would be filled with pitfalls.

It's Sunday!

CHAPTER SIXTEEN
Journey to Recovery

My family continued to struggle; not only financially, but emotionally as well. Sure, couples were entering the world of matrimony, and obligating themselves to a lifetime commitment. Still divorce and separation was on the rise. Not only in the Black community, but every nationality was having a hard time maintaining their marital status. Therefore, my battle was not uncommon.

After eighteen years, Gerald finally lost interest in our relationship, and I was feeling the results. "Gerald, you're not spending enough time with me. When exactly are we going out again? It's been months since we've gone anywhere."

" Sunday. I just took you out last month. I do have to work and make a living, ya know. Things have been kinda slow at the shop. What do you want me to do, huh? You wanted more money, so I gotta work.

You stepped into this with your eyes wide open."

Yes. Due to the shortage of income in our house, we felt Gerald should extend his hours of operation. Time from home left me feeling lonely and confused. Most couples would be proud of nineteen years of marriage. Our daughter had just graduated from high school. Now, I felt trapped with no way out.

I'd lost my identity, and neglected my singing career. Yes, I continued to sing and to direct the church choir. Every now and then, I sang at weddings. Now, my heart was occupied in other matters.

My focus was a burning desire for companionship. God had taken a backseat in my life. As my environment grew cold, bitterness swelled inside me. I found no pleasure with myself, or those around me. There was no interest in singing in the mirror. Time spent in God's presence was sporadic. Through the years, my family depended on me. Everyone's needs were before my own. Who was I? Furthermore, who had I become?

It's Sunday!

Clad in my robe, I sat at the breakfast table. I raised a spoon filled with cereal to my lips. Nigel had strolled into the kitchen. "It's about time you got going."

Nigel pulled pancakes from the microwave and stacked them neatly. Much like his father's, his shoulders spanned the length of the double doors on the kitchen cabinet. My little Nigel was turning into a man. Following his parent's musical footsteps, he loved music and thrived on it. "Should I drop you off at rehearsal?"

"No, mama," He replied, in a profound masculine voice. Afterward he loaded a knife with butter, then smeared it on the second layer of his pancakes. "May I use your car tonight?"

I put down my spoon and frowned. "Better ask your dad. You know how he is."

Nigel placed his plate on the table and turned to get the syrup from the cabinet. "He let Tuesday use it."

"Yeah, but Tuesday is older."

"Unfair. Like usual." He shoved his thumb in his mouth to remove the excess butter, and then he picked up a warm skillet from the stove.

I sighed. "…coming home for dinner tonight?"

"Nah." Taking his fork, he raked fried eggs from the skillet and onto his plate. "I'll grab a taco or something." He sat down at the table beside me.

"Nigel. You've spilled something on your shirt." I reached over to brush at the dried stain. Nigel grasped my hand, and suspended it in midair.

"I'll take care of it," he whispered. "I wash my own clothes, remember. I know how to pretreat a stain."

Noting the authority in his voice, I withdrew. "Well. Excuse me."

"What time did dad get home last night?"

I sighed. "Well. You know your dad. He was late as usual."

Nigel reached for his juice, his large hands wrapped around the tiny glass. He took a sip. "Mama." He exhaled loudly. "I think you need to get a life."

It's Sunday!

I lowered my brows, then looked over my glasses. "Excuse you. What did you say little boy?"

"I mean, you never go anywhere. You don't talk on the phone anymore. When I came home last night you were sitting in the living room."

"So." I shrugged, and picked up my coffee. "What's wrong with that?"

"Mama." He looked at me with dark narrowed eyes. "In the dark? The television wasn't even on."

"Well, you guys don't seem to need me anymore. This house used to be alive with screaming kids, music, and fun. Now it's quiet and kinda lonely."

"I know." As he chewed his food, his temples throbbed.

"So. Mr. Psychologist. Where do I go from here? Tuesday is in college, now. It was hard to leave her. I had tears in my eyes, a lump in my throat, and pain in my heart."

"Yeah, I knew you were hiding your tears. You aren't very good at it, you know."

"Yesterday, Tuesday was just a little girl. She loved playing dolls with her pink, plastic playhouse." I drew in a breath. "That was the best Christmas present ever. You were her only playmate." I elevated my arm to rest my chin on my palm. "Don't you miss her?"

"Sure." He speared his eggs and raised them to his mouth. "I'm not home much, but it's kinda nice."

"Your dad pretended he couldn't make the trip." I folded my arms. "I knew he couldn't deal with losing his daughter."

"You had a hard time too, Mom. But, we were there for you."

"Yeah, I know." I pushed my cereal aside. "While I was driving home, all I could think about was the past—all the arguments, the fights, and the spanking you guys got."

"Yeah. Tuesday was one of the loudest sopranos in the Youth Choir, you know. You guys are going to miss her."

"I know. Plus, I don't know what your cousins are going to do. She was everyone's hair dresser."

It's Sunday!

Nigel poured extra syrup on his pancakes. "Leave it to dad to give her an old mannequin head. What else was she going to learn to do? Hair and singing is in her blood."

"You're right." I closed my robe tightly. "It gets kinda lonely around here. You're at practice, Tuesday is having fun at college, and your dad is always busy."

Hearing dogs barking, Nigel paused. He turned and gazed out the kitchen window. "I'll bet that dog is out again."

I took in my son's fresh haircut, and his neatly groomed appearance. Then I looked into his face. "You're dark around the eyes, son. You look tired. You need to get to bed earlier. Stop spending so much time on that computer and phone. I'll bet you keep yourself busy to avoid thinking about your sister."

"Man." He shrugged. "You just don't know. I'm just busy."

Whether he wanted it or not, Nigel had finally gotten the house to himself. I wasn't sure what our lives would be like after Tuesday left for college.

CHAPTER SEVENTEEN
Let No Man Put Asunder

Parents want the best for their children. This includes college, marriage, and a wonderful career. However, our lives are filled with generational curses that must be bound in Jesus's name. Walking in my mother's shoes, I also felt the sting and disappointment of parenting. Less than a year later, Tuesday delivered a package from college that would change our lives forever.

A frail and confused young woman moved back home. Because God is gracious, Tuesday gave birth to a beautiful son. God is merciful and forgiving. He gave her strength to get a job, continue her studies, and raise her son.

Once again, thoughts of divorce were on my mind. Our communication was skewed. Arguments over finances, jealousy, and neglect, kept our home in a constant uproar.

It's Sunday!

I figured I earned pretty good wages. Even so, I felt guilty if I needed anything for myself. From birth, I was a giver, never taking into account my own comfort.

One day, as I drove down the freeway. A profound thought struck me. I loved God, believed in God, and talked to God. But, we are flesh, and humans need physical interaction. When God fashioned Adam, he said it was not good for man to be alone. How was my life any different? I needed someone I could depend on, and yet I felt utterly alone.

Gerald was extremely talented. I felt he needed to get another degree, but in computer technology, graphic, and designs. For years, I watched him stay up late working on computers. Obviously, technology was the gift God had given him. Why bury your talent?

My father woke up early and left for work. He was a loving man who was patient and kind—was I asking for too much after almost twenty years of marriage?

Rehashing the same old quarrels was wearing me down. I questioned God. Does true love really exist? Is there genuine, love on this earth?

* * * * *

My children were on their own. So, I needed to occupy myself by finding new interests. There was no joy in my soul. How long had it been since I laughed out loud? God had blessed me with a wonderful job, a great family, a nurturing church, and loving friends. Several times, I left home. Did I really want to continue my relationship with my husband? Years of disagreements had caused numerous physical ailments. Was I falling completely apart?

The bible says, *A man shall leave his father and mother and cleave to his wife, and they two shall become one flesh*. It also says, *What God has joined together, let no man put asunder*. Did I actually put my own marriage together? Were we unequally yoked? Then I leaned on the scripture, *An unbelieving spouse is sanctified by the believing spouse*.

It's Sunday!

Concerning my husband, I didn't notice a change in his behavior. All of his habits remained the same. I can't say Gerald was not *real* with God. Yet, I prayed that God would save him, and grant him eternal life.

CHAPTER EIGHTEEN
The Pig Pen Phase

The phone rang, disturbing my pity party. I rolled over in the bed and grasped the handset. From the caller ID, I could see that it was Wanda calling. "Hey Wanda."

"Sunday," Wanda demanded cheerfully, "girl, you'd better get outta that bed. Its girl's night."

I twisted my mouth pensively. "No. I don't think so. I just don't feel like it."

"I'll bet you have on that same old raggedly house dress. Don't you? Girl, you act like you're dead. It's only 8:00 and you're already asleep."

"I wasn't asleep. Just thinking."

"You think too much. You need to get out of that house. It's 8:00 on a Friday night, my friend. Take a shower, then slide that cute little pant suit on your booty."

"No." A television sat on the dresser; I turned my attentions to a popular rerun.

It's Sunday!

"Where is the Sunday I use to know? You're gonna rot in that bed. I'll be there shortly. And, if you're not ready to go, I'm gonna drag you out in that stinky old house dress."

The thought of Wanda dragging me against my will made me chuckle. "Okay, Miss Thang."

Dressing up did make me feel better. I hadn't gone to a club in years. Right away, I became new meat on the scene. Men liked what they saw. To them, I was not just some stale, played-out housewife. I was beautiful, vivacious, and alive!

Time after time, men approached our table. I loved the attention of their harmless flirting. All night, I fought unwanted advances. Soon, I became a junky. It didn't matter how old they were, their slippery words filled a void in my life. As long as I was not sleeping with these men, I wasn't cheating, right?

From that day forth, I realized I needed this attention fix. Dopamine made my face glow with excitement. Unfortunately, after a few months, I became the prodigal son.

Though I didn't drink, a riotous lifestyle consumed me. There was no way I'd step out on my husband. But mentally, I loved the thought of men clamoring to get my attention. Their voices were smooth; their lies soothing to my ears.

Soon, I hit rock bottom. Thoughts of infidelity were growing inside me. What started as a harmless game was ending badly. I was becoming so weak; I knew I'd find myself in the arms of one of these players.

Was I entering the pigpen phase? Yes. Filled with remorse, I returned home. I told my husband I didn't want to destroy my family. Then, I waited on God's will for my life. Gerald assured me that he still loved me, and wanted to make the marriage work.

With counseling from our pastor, we agreed to live according to God's standards. We went forth with our marriage. My husband decided to reunite with the church.

It's Sunday!

We acknowledge that God has to be the ultimate head of the relationship. God first, family next, education, and business last. There is no doubt that God will give us strength in our time of trials.

Going thru disagreements and heartaches, I found myself escaping to my secret place. As a child, I found solace in my bathroom. I'd sing in the mirror until the stress melted away.

Being an adult, when tension slammed me against the wall, I'd sing my heart out. With a hung head, and a heavy heart, I'd once again, pick up my hair bush. Using this trusty microphone, I'd sing loud and clear. ♫"Even though I can't see, and I can't feel your touch, I will trust you Lord...." Tears would stream down my cheek. By doing this, my sorrow would always turn to rejoicing.

* * * * *

As time went on, our relationship returned to normal. To enhance our marriage, we spent time together. After Sunday's services, Gerald would relax in front of the television.

Sometimes, I would lay my head in his lap, as he loved watching his old movies.

Needing a little excitement, I looked into Gerald's face. His gaze was constant; his eyes danced from movie scene, to movie scene.

I raised my head from his lap. "Gerald."

"Yeah," he answered absently.

"Let's go bike riding, or walking? We need to get out of the house."

Pretending to dodge a blow, Gerald jerked his head to one side. "Man! That's gotta hurt," he remarked, talking to the television set. "Maybe later. I'm resting now."

As I knew so well, later would never come. I rolled over on my side and cradled my face against his thigh. Remembering my near fate with adultery, I then settled down.

* * * * *

Gerald was always one to stay busy. He engaged in house projects—fixing and destroying things around the house, all at the same time.

It's Sunday!

I learned to appreciate his interest in learning new things. He always acted as if he'd worked on something like that before. Standing before scattered debris from a broken stove, I'd ask, "Gerald have you ever fixed something like this before?"

His answer was always the same. "Man, yeah. I used to fix these long time ago."

I believed in Gerald's natural talent. There wasn't anything he couldn't fix. "I don't know Gerald. We might need to call a repairman."

The word *repairman,* was the ultimate insult to Gerald. It usually riled his dander. "Why should I pay somebody else to fix it, when I can fix it myself?"

His specialty was fixing lawn mowers, bicycles, light fixtures, computers, house appliances, and cars. Of these traits, he had given several to his daughter.

With that confidence, she could achieve any chosen goal.

Sunday Stepney Lewis

No matter how hard we tried, things just didn't work out. In less than two months, I found myself making an appointment to see a divorce attorney. Twenty years of marriage, had not come easy. There was no trust. Gerald started accusing me of seeing men, and I accused him as well.

The internet, and cell phones had been corrosive to our marriage, and trust waned. Jealousy reared its ugly head, and I found myself envious of his female clientele.

Revenge clouded my judgment. Once again, mentally, I stepped outside my marriage. I needed attention from someone, and anyone would do. Women flitted around Gerald, but I didn't care anymore.

Short of getting into bed, I was getting what I needed outside my marriage. Flirting with a fantasy was not cheating, right? To these men, I was a diamond. My body was tight, and my eyes sparkled like jewels. Every now and then, I needed to hear how wonderful and special Sunday was.

It's Sunday!

Clearly, it was time for a divorce. A promotion on my job gave me the strength to believe I could take care of myself. Though my life was a shambles, I continued to trust in God. He would provide for us.

CHAPTER NINETEEN
Day of Awakening

At age forty-four, I found myself signing divorce papers. I moved in with my sister for three months. This time, our marriage was finally over. We went before the court system and finalized our divorce in September 2010.

Nigel and I finally moved into our own apartment. Things were looking up, however past scares haunted me. A divorce should have made life easier, right? So, why couldn't I simply bounce back? There were lots of mental hang-ups, and numerous trust issues. These feelings were not normal, nor were they acceptable. I needed a healing from God.

Didn't I have a life before marriage? Why couldn't I grasp the golden ring? Once, I was an active person; singing, going out with friends, and interacting with people in general.

Now, all I did was go to church, and work. I started to sleep my life away. The next day, the same routine started over again, and again.

It's Sunday!

How did I get to this place of solitude, loneliness, and void?

Nigel had finished two years at a community college. Now, it was time for him to venture off, and further his education at a university. Although I was happy, a sense of selfishness, and sadness engulfed me. My son was going to leave me alone.

* * * * *

One of the biggest arguments that Gerald and I had was about married men. In the heat of an argument, Gerald would say, "When you're not with me anymore, married men will approach you. Watch and see!"

"You a liar," I scolded. "God's got somebody out there for me. He's gonna love me the right way. Just you wait and see."

I didn't understand how Gerald came to this conclusion. However, when you're trying to do right there's always temptation — especially when you're married.

I admitted that men approached me. Starved for affection, it wasn't always easy to decline their offers. But, there are always consequences to our actions. Either they will be positive, or negative.

Humorously, I decided that Facebook was a work of the devil—of that, I was sure. Actually, blaming Facebook for breaking up marriages is like blaming a gun for killing a person. Someone had to pull the trigger, right?

After our divorce, I found that Gerald's words were true. Indeed, numerous married men approached me. They made advances in the name of friendship. Their pretense was to encourage me—help me through my lonely hours. "How are you holding up," they'd ask, and "how are you really doing?"

The truth had finally come out. I was the damsel in distress, on the rebound, and an easy target.

As I lay in my bed, I wondered what happened to Tim, Jim, and Slim—all the single guys I fought off when I was married.

It's Sunday!

Satan knows when you're most vulnerable and easily influenced.

My so-called friends suddenly changed their conversation to, "Hello Beautiful. How are you, sexy? I gotta get wit you, woman." So, these were my so called, friends? No my friends *didn't* ask me out on a date. There was *not* a night on the town. Suddenly, I simply became *a booty call.*

They wanted to hang out at my place. Word spread quickly that Sunday was available, and on the market. Yes, I wanted to interact with men, but I also needed time to heal.

* * * * *

One day, I got a message from an old friend through Facebook. My long, lost friend, Shawn Davis, was still around. *Hello, Ms. Sunday. Shawn Davis here. Do you remember me? It's been a long time. I saw your picture on Face Book and decided to speak to you. Are you still singing? Made any records lately?*

Tears plumped in my eyes. I often wondered what happened to Shawn.

After all these years, his note was refreshing.

I responded, *Yes Shawn. I do remember you.* My heart raced with excitement. Where was he in his life? Was he also single? Shawn mentioned that he lived in another state. He would be coming to town on business.

Immediately I insisted, "Maybe, you can come by the church and hear me sing. It's been so long."

"I'll call you when I get in town."

After the conversation, I realized I forgot to ask if he was married, so I texted him. His answer was, *I'll tell you when I get there.*

So, you're trying to be funny, I replied, wary of his vague answer. I placed a call to him. "Surely you wouldn't agree to see me if you're married, would you?"

A chuckle sifted from the phone. "She won't be coming with us. It will be the boys and me. After all, we're just old friends."

Hearing the term *friends*, I cringed. *Here we go again.*

It's Sunday!

"There's nothing wrong seeing an old friend, right? Believe me there are no strings attached."

Exasperated, I sighed. "You know how I am about seeing married men."

Shawn assured me that our visit would be innocent. First of all, I had invited him to church. How could it possibly turn into a date?

Just as Shawn promised, he indeed called when he arrived in town. Now, he wanted to meet at a nearby restaurant and I agreed.

No problem, I told myself, he lives out of town. After our dinner, we'll go our separate ways. Totally innocent. When I walked into the restaurant, he was waiting at a table. We had both matured gracefully. At least, that's how I felt.

Shawn stood as I neared the table. He seemed even taller and more handsome than ever. The last time I saw Shawn, he was dressed in suit and tie.

Now, years later, a smartly tailored suit fit perfect across his broad shoulders.

Thick lashes were still the highlight of his signature look. A smile dimpled his tawny cheeks, and exposed faint character lines beside his hazel eyes. Caught in his spell, I felt my face redden. Was I all that he expected? I placed my arms around his neck, and tiptoed to hug him. "Shawn."

"Hello stranger." Immediately, Shawn's mellow voice pierced my heart. Education and breeding had given him an air of authority. Confidence poured from his very being. He held me at arm's length and studied my face. "It's been a long time."

Was I dreaming? For some reason I didn't know how to respond. A bad case of the jitters rested in the pit of my stomach. When Shawn hugged me again, I scanned the restaurant searching for church members, classmates, and friends. Then a startling thought struck me. I'm not married anymore. Even so, being with Shawn made me feel inadequate.

Shawn placed his fingers beneath my chin and turned my face toward his.

It's Sunday!

Engaging my eyes he asked, "You aren't nervous are you?"

Feeling the warmth of his fingers against my face, I blushed again. "Just a little."

He pulled out a chair and calmness flowed over me. "Twenty-five years is a long time, lady. We have much to talk about."

While we ate our meal, Shawn gave me semisweet smiles. Every word from his curvaceous lips caused my stomach to tighten. Though I went through the gestures, I could hardly eat.

Soon, Shawn wiped his mouth and placed his napkin aside. He expelled a long sigh, grasped my hand, then gave a gentle squeeze. Raising a brow, he spoke. "Sunday. Sunday. Just look at you. After all these years, you still make my heart race." He shook his head, and his curly hair glistened in the evening sun. "You meant so much to me. When you walked out of my life, I knew you *didn't* feel the same. At that time, I couldn't give you what you wanted, or what you needed.

We were both starving artists." Shawn cocked his head to one side. "Remember Lisa Johnson — our classmate."

Recalling Lisa very well, I nodded. "Don't tell me she's your wife."

"For fifteen years, Sunday. Well, last year I found out she had an affair with my cousin. You remember Jeff, don't you?"

Once again, I nodded, hardly able to breath.

"Well. I did my best to make this marriage work. Nothing was ever enough. She hurt me, Sunday." He shook his head. "I'm still trying to forgive her. I'm trying to pick up the pieces. It hasn't been easy."

Was Shawn also looking for attention elsewhere? Or, was it a payback ploy? "I'm sorry to hear that. You deserve so much better. Believe me — I do understand your pain." I looked down at the sun-deprived skin where my wedding ring once adorned my finger.

"You know, Shawn. God created the heart.

He won't allow more than we can bear. Seek God for your answer."

After dinner, the night was still early. We decided to sit and talk. The night melted away in a river of splendor. No matter what we were discussing, I hung on Shawn's every word.

Was this the man I needed in my life? Why was I enjoying Shawn's company now? When we were younger, I had every opportunity to date him, but I didn't. I took in Shawn's chiseled features. His dreamy eyes were breathtaking; I wanted to kick myself. This man wanted me—at the time, what was I thinking?

As the night waned, departure was upon us. I didn't want to see him leave. Nevertheless, Shawn was married, and someone I needed to forget. The happiness of his marriage was important to me as well. My struggles had taught me *not* to interfere with forgiveness. Yes, it was nice to see Shawn, with his rich hazel eyes. I wished him well, and we parted.

That initial contact with Shawn was one of many. We talked on the phone and I won't deny enjoying his conversations. Dare I admit I was hooked? I watched my caller ID constantly. At any given time, I was never far from his communication. I had given Shawn all means to contact me.

Now, I had to hear his voice. Was I becoming obsessed with someone else's husband? I'd replay my voice mail repeatedly just to get my fix.

This was the devil's temptation and I had no control. Suddenly, Shawn's attention was what I lived for. I felt comfortable, and loved. There were times he had to rush off the phone, or cut our conversations short. Somehow, this became my fantasy world.

One night Shawn called. "Sunday, I'll be flying in this weekend. I thought we could visit for a while. Will you be available?"

Naturally, I looked forward to his visits. "I guess so. I'll check my schedule. Let me see if I can make arrangements." Though I tried to hide my feelings, I was desperately into him.

It's Sunday!

A man, I overlooked many years ago, seemed to be all the man I needed.

"I'll call you when I arrive."

This time, when Shawn came to town, there was no question where we'd meet. We were both secure with when and where. No distractions. I waited in front of our meeting place.

Finally, Shawn arrived. Something was different about him. "Hey," he said grinning, "how's Sunday?"

Yes, there was something strange about him. And yes, this visit would be different. Because we had discussed our feelings, I was more at ease, and relaxed.

"Shawn." Annoyed with our present location, I searched his eyes. "Why don't we talk at my place? It's quiet there."

Appearing puzzled, Shawn turned his head slightly. He ran his eyes over my body. "Are you sure about that?"

I wasn't sure, but I wanted any part of Shawn I could get. "Yes."

Getting back into his car, Shawn then followed me to my house. When we walked toward my front door, he placed his hand in the small of my back.

Right then, an innocent visit took on a more intimate tone. As soon as we entered the living room, Shawn closed the door behind us. He grabbed me around the waist, and pulled me near.

Pressing my body against the front door, he gently caressed my form. After kissing me, Shawn brushed his thumbs against my sensitive lips. "You feel so good in my arms. This—this is where you belong."

Already it was difficult for me to pull away. I had fallen in love with him. "Shawn." I removed his hand and kissed it. "I'm so sorry. We can't do this."

Shawn narrowed his eyes. Passion smoldered as he planted kisses along my neck. His desire was ignited, as his breathing had grown erratic. "Sunday," he crooned.

"For years, I've thought of nothing but you. You were the big fish who got away from Shawn Lamar Davis.

There's no way I can walk away from you, now. I need you." There was desperation in his eyes. "Sunday.

It's Sunday!

If you don't show me to your room, I'll swear I'll make love to you—right here, and right now." He nodded to assure me of his intensions.

Starved, helpless, and weak as I was, I took Shawn by the hand, then, led him to paradise. Together, we were perfect. This experience would linger in my mind, as one I'd never forget. However, after drifting from our mountain, reality hit hard. There was a moment of silence. We had done the unthinkable! Inside, my heart was crushed. Gerald's words rang out in my memory. Married men. You watch. Married men are going after you. They'll use you and hurt you. Watch what I tell you.

With Gerald's words echoing in my head, I pulled the sheets around my body, then turned my back to Shawn.

Seeming to sense my concern, he comforted me. "Sunday." He touched my shoulder, and I winced. "Sunday. Don't worry. I know we've done wrong. Baby. Don't do this to us. God is merciful.

He'll forgive us." Shawn turned my body to face his.

"I won't leave you, Sunday.

We'll pray, and ask God for his guidance. If we're faithful he will deliver us."

I pushed against Shawn's warm, bare chest. "Shawn. We knew better. We walked into this with both eyes open. God is not someone you can bargain with, when it's convenient for you."

Shawn's lips parted. He appeared confused—speechless. "Sunday."

"No. Shawn." I removed his hand and pushed him away. "God won't help us. This is not his will." I pulled myself to an upright position. "The spirit is not going to allow this. We will be held accountable. The wages of sin is death."

It's Sunday!

CHAPTER TWENTY
Sunday's Sun Shine

There were still obstacles I had to face. My son's college education took priority. Now, my children depended on me, no matter where they were. Tuesday grew up. Working, and having a young child, she was overwhelmed with many responsibilities. Her primary concern was her son. However, singing, and acting, brought her much joy. Obviously, the cycle started again. This time, fate fell on the shoulders of my precious daughter. Tuesday had been an actress all her life. As a child, she sang and loved acting. Church plays, school plays and community plays totally excited her.

As miracles unfold, a young man named Andre walked into her life. "Mama," she said, in a giddy tone. "I want you to meet my friend, Andre. Mama. He's just like me. He wants to be a singer and an actor too."

Tuesday and Andre traveled the world auditioning, and pursuing their dreams.

Andre was getting serious about my spirited daughter.

When Andre looked at Tuesday, there was magic in his eyes. There was no doubt, he loved her.

Now, I understood the lament of his longing expression. It was the dream all mothers have for their daughter. The blissful scent of commitment was in the air. Andre wanted to wed my daughter, and I couldn't have approved more. Someone still believed in love and marriage.

Tuesday made wedding plans for her big day. Excited, I helped as much as I could. This was my baby girl. Hopefully, this would be the only wedding ceremony she'd ever have. That is to say, trust God, and there will be no divorce.

The day of the wedding finally arrived. Tuesday's dress was beautiful — designed with a strapless, laced top. It was the most stunning gown I'd ever seen.

It's Sunday!

Reverend Stepney, Tuesday's uncle, stood before them. "Who gives this bride away?"

After a few seconds, her father stood. "I do."

Tuesday gazed lovingly at her father, and then smiled.

Gerald laced his fingers, and placed his hand neatly before him. "If you don't mind, reverend. I have something to say to my beautiful daughter."

With widened eyes, Tuesday's smile faded. She nodded.

"Tuesday. You have been the sunshine of my life. Right now, I want you to know, that your creation was an act of love." He turned to address the congregation. "As you all know, for the past couple of years, my family has gone through trying times. But, through it all, we taught our children to do the right thing. With permission from my daughter, and my soon to be son, I would like to ask her mother, Sunday, to stand."

Hearing my name, an electrical shock ran down my spine. I looked up in total confusion.

My sister was sitting next to me. "What in the world is he doing?" Embarrassed to no end, I stood with tears in my eyes. Why was he interrupting our daughter's ceremony?

"Sunday," he called. "I still love you. I know it hasn't been easy for you. I'm sorry for all the changes, and all the hardships we've encountered in our family's life.

Right now, I'd like to ask that you forgive me. I also ask that you take my hand in marriage. Trust me, once more. Please."

Gerald's eyes held a pleading stare, and everyone was gawking. What was I going to say? Seconds passed slowly. Perspiration beaded on my forehead. Turning to my right, I looked at my mother. Then, I turned my gaze straight ahead to look at my daughter. Her expression was one of concern. Next, I sought the face of my son. No one gave me the sign I was looking for.

Beneath the lovely corsage, my heart beat wildly. Confused and torn, a tear rolled down my cheek.

It's Sunday!

Before I knew it, tears were streaming. Holding the hem of my dress, I rushed down the aisle, and then burst through the closed entrance. Once in the foyer, I sat down on a padded chair and cried. Others had followed, and stood above me. Immediately, the pastor restored order and took charge of the service.

After clearing his throat, he proceeded with the wedding ceremony. How could I miss my daughter's wedding? Gathering my strength, I stood. From the window on the door, I looked toward the front of the church.

Her father was now seated; he held his head in his hands. Yes. Gerald had opened the coffin that held our marriage; mixed emotions had surfaced with a vengeance.

* * * * *

I couldn't see myself with Gerald. Instead, I continued to seek guidance and directions from God. Satan's ears are always listening — waiting to intervene.

Distraught, I ask God if there was refuge for me.

Can anyone love me the way Christ loved the church?

My father always taught me, that a good name is better than any riches. Is there some type of significance by my name being, Sunday? Was Sunday really more than just a day of the week? Yes, Sunday is one of God's creations with a divine plan over her life. I prayed that God would reward me for trying to be sincere, not perfect, but sincere.

It's Sunday!

CHAPTER TWENTY-ONE
Wake-up and Live!

Lunch with Braden, my older brother, had been enjoyable. Because he lived so far away, I hardly saw him. Our frank conversation helped me to focus. Yes, I was headed for the bright lights. What happened to that girl with the golden voice? Dressed in sweatpants, I sat on the side of the bed reminiscing about my past. Braden's wisdom had caused me to question my life.

Pictures were, tangled, and sprawled on my bedspread. My children had grown up fast. I marveled at Nigel's height against his father. The last album held my hopes and dreams. I reached for it with anticipation. What would I find? It had been years since I turned the pages and saw myself on stage.

Immediately, dried petals fell from the pages and landed on my spread. Instantly, I smiled.

It was the pink rose Shawn had given me all those years ago. The frilly pink ribbon had turned brown. I cleaned up the petals thinking of my decision to dismiss Shawn from my life.

It had been six months since we spoke. Times were difficult. Most men were dogs, or married. Either way Sunday had no one.

A sigh sifted from my chest. Though I was lonely, I knew I did the right thing. Surely, God was pleased. I cast my gaze upwards and smiled. To God be the glory. Shawn had left unbelievable battle scars. Now they were healing. I lifted the next page studying the neatness of my small figure.

My phone rang, breaking my concentration. The caller ID lit up brightly. "Shawn." Weak to hear his voice, I snatched the phone from the cradle. "Hello, Mr. Davis."

"Hello, Sunday. My, my. You sound cheery this evening."

"I had a fantastic day. How are you?"

"I'm good." He paused. "Eh, I was wondering if…"

"No."

"I was going to ask if you…"

"No. No. Shawn. I won't see you. Not now, or ever. Not as long as you're married to Lisa. I'm not going to sleep feeling guilty anymore. Do you understand that?"

Shawn chuckled. "Yes, Sunday. I do understand. I have something for you."

"Shawn Davis. I'm not falling for that. Do you think I'm a stupid teenager?"

"Hardly. You're all woman."

"Funny," I added nodding.

"Really. I need to talk to you."

"And, I'm hanging up the phone right now."

"Please don't."

"Give me one good reason why I should continue our conversation?"

"I have one. I promise I won't try anything. I'm on the level."

"I swear if you try anything, I'm going to kiss your lips, then kick you out of my door."

"Why so drastic?" he chuckled. "I cross my heart I'll stay in line."

Shawn was on his way and I rushed to get ready. Seems there was not enough time for me to turn into a diva. I decided to remain casual, but fresh. Before I knew it, there was a knock on my door. My stomach knotted. Would I be strong enough to fight my feelings for him? I moistened my lips and opened the door. Immediately, I rushed into his arms. "I hate you."

He kissed the tip of my nose. "But. I love you."

I narrowed my eyes in warning. "Shawn."

"Let's sit down. Just to show you I'm on the level, let's sit at the table."

"You said you had something for me." I opened his blazer. "Did you lie?"

"No. I have it right here." Shawn reached into the pocket of his suit. He pulled out an envelope.

"What is it?" I was curious and he knew it.

He gave it to me. "Open it."

Quickly, I opened the envelope. I read the flyer inside. "This says that Tyler Perry is holding auditions here.

Wow. How did you find out?"

"I have connections."

I shook my head, gave the envelope back, then backed away. "Once upon a time, Shawn. Those days are over."

"Sunday. I believe in you. I pulled a few strings. Only a few people will audition. Guess what? You're among that few."

"What are you saying?" I asked, raising a brow.

"I'm saying that, I know a person, who knows a person. These people have already heard your voice. I gave them the CD we made a few months ago." Shawn shrugged. "There are a few others, but mostly someone is interested in hearing you."

"Tell me you're kidding." I plopped down on a chair.

"Tyler Perry heard me sing?"

Shawn shook his head. "No, but your chances at the audition are really good."

A glow warmed my face. "How wonderful!"

That's not all. I have more news."

"Nothing could top this, Shawn. That's a dream come true."

"Well, I'm in the mood for granting wishes."

"Okay. Tell me." I giggled, and folded the flyer.

Turning from my view, Shawn walked toward the living room. "Sunday. Come here. Let's sit on the sofa."

"Shawn," I warned once more.

"No. I promise." He raised both hands.

Once I was seated, Shawn started. "Lisa ran away with Jeff."

"What!" The shock made me sit up straight.

"Yes. She divorced me."

"Really? I'm so sorry." Inside I was dancing. "When did this happen?"

"The last time I saw you, I went home to an empty house. Lisa had taken the boys and left the state. Seems Jeff also disappeared at that same time."

"O. M. G."

"I took off from work. While I was cleaning up the mess, our divorce papers arrived."

"Wow."

"My divorce was final three months ago." He lowered his gaze.

Tears stood in my eyes. "What? Why didn't you call me?"

"Well, Sunday. Much like you. I needed time to heal. My boys mean the world to me. I stopped loving Lisa long ago. But, right is right. She was pregnant with our oldest son when we got married. I was trying to do the right thing. After all, she didn't get pregnant by herself."

"Shawn. No."

He sighed. "I'd like to see you again."

"If I said I didn't want to see you. I would be telling a lie."

"Sunday." He kissed my lips. "Take a chance.

You've let me walk out of your life too many times. Give me a try. I believe I can make you happy."

At that moment, I fell into Shawn's arms. We made a commitment to take things slow. One day at a time.

* * * * *

God allowed me to go through transitions in my life. Through my experiences, I am able to touch the spirits of others. People believe in God, but at times, they need physical encouragement. Most trials are temporary. You must experience them in order to grow — to get to the place God wants you to be. When a problem is repetitious, find out what God is trying to show you. Only then, can you elevate to a higher level.

Satan loves torment, worry, and depression, of which God is neither. When dealing with problems, exercise your faith. God will always show you his perfect will for your life. Faith is the substance of things hoped for and the evidence of things that are unseen, Hebrews 11:1.

~End~

It's Sunday!

About the Author
Sunday Stepney Lewis

Sunday Stepney Lewis is a proud Texas native. At her Grandmother's behest, Sunday's weekday name was given. She loves to sing, write, and enjoys playing the piano. Born last of nine siblings, Sunday refused to hide her powerful voice among her talented brothers and sisters. A bratty little girl grows up and paves her way through the cruel music industry. Along her journey, she finds heartache, pain, triumph, and redemption.

Inspirational, Christian, E-books & Print
Topaz Books!
http://www.topazpublishingllc.com
sundaystepneylewis.com